Picking the Bones of Eleven Presidents and Others

By a Journalist with Presidential Credentials

JERRY MORIARITY

Edited by Dr. Diane Holloway

iUniverse, Inc.
New York   Bloomington

Picking the Bones of Eleven Presidents and Others
By a Journalist with Presidential Credentials

iUniverse books may be ordered through booksellers or by contacting:

iUniverse
1663 Liberty Drive
Bloomington, IN 47403
www.iuniverse.com
1-800-Authors (1-800-288-4677)

Because of the dynamic nature of the Internet, any Web addresses or
links contained in this book may have changed since publication and
may no longer be valid. The views expressed in this work are solely those
of the author and do not necessarily reflect the views of the publisher,
and the publisher hereby disclaims any responsibility for them.

978-1-4401-0711-5 (sc)
978-1-4401-0712-2 (ebook)

Printed in the United States of America

iUniverse rev. date: 12/19/2008

Dedication

To my devoted wife, Betty (Dr. Elizabeth), whose earnest loyalty and counsel were more than I deserved.

To my eight children, their spouses and grandchildren, who brightened my life in ways I never dreamed possible.

To my many fallen Air Force buddies who sacrificed so generously to make the United States a great and free country.

And to the many dedicated leaders and interesting personalities who became subjects for chapters of this publication.

Acknowledgements

I want to thank Dick Riniker of *La Crosse Tribune* for doing the photo of myself which I used at the back of this book.

I very much appreciate the help of Janice Beals (A Designer's Touch) who prepared the photos and created the book cover.

I would also like to thank my editor, Dr. Diane Holloway, who wrote and/or edited *Dallas and the Jack Ruby Trial, The Mind of Oswald, Autobiography of Lee Harvey Oswald, Jack Ruby, American History Through Songs, Who Killed New Orleans, Jacuzzi,* and other books.

Illustrations

Table of Contents

PART FOUR Not All Malarkey Essays

Postscript After Death Story

Introduction

How It Started

Roy L. Bangsberg, editor of *The Tribune* in La Crosse, Wisconsin, hired me on St. Patrick's Day (March 17, 1941)—a gigantic break just before World War II. That was great for a kid whose career began with an imagined interview with Samuel Clemens (Mark Twain) written in high school. The piece was noticed by an exec at WKBH (which we called the Why Kick Be Happy station) who wanted it adapted for radio use. Next, I became sports editor and columnist of the *Aquinas News,* which somehow convinced Sister Bernice that I should be the next editor of the *Aquinas News,* which then won All-American honors and led to my job with *The Tribune.*

Employment at *The Tribune* provided many new opportunities. Wisconsin was a hot bed for politics, and politicians and candidates criss-crossed the state often. Editor Bangsberg favored me with assignments.

The big adventure, of course, was the assignment to ride on President Harry Truman's presidential campaign train through Minnesota and Wisconsin. I believe I was the only one to get an interview and a photo op with Truman on the train. I'll describe that later.

Truman was Number One in the parade of eleven presidents that I have interviewed and photographed during my career. My parents also took me to see Franklin Delano Roosevelt, but I was much too young for an interview.

After interviewing all the presidents from Harry Truman on down to the present, I began to imagine the ideal U.S. President. Even though I have had more than 40 interviews and photo opportunities with the last 11 presidents, I felt honor-bound to dissect each office holder and select their more favorable traits. These topics created my study of the presidents, which has been my hobby for some fifty years.

There has been so much negativity about the people who occupy the highest throne in the free world that it's surprising that so many individuals campaign so vigorously. With all the hardships a President has to endure, you sometimes wonder why anyone aspires to the office.

Just think through the years, four presidents have been assassinated and many more have been targets of assassinations. More or less, we've enjoyed a free society in this country. However, terrorists and malcontents are making it exceedingly difficult to ignore the viruses of anti-government discontent.

Strange, isn't it, that we can walk on the moon, but not in our own neighborhoods? Somehow, we live closer together but farther apart. We can build libraries, schools, community centers, churches, even football stadiums, but we can't close the gaps of intolerance, indifference and prejudice. Knowledge should be, but is not, enough. Those who know right, do wrong. Despite all the problems, I remain an optimist and I will be thankful to those who make good things happen.

I am reminded of a little known but beautiful inscription, which adorned the desk of President John F. Kennedy. It read: "Oh, God, Thy sea is so great…and my boat is so small."

All presidents must have felt the same intimidation while in office, but can all the citizens of this country look back always with pride on how we have rocked the boat?

Egotism being what it is, presidential candidates continue to contend with each other, so I will expound upon my thoughts for the ideal president.

Creating an Ideal President

If I want to create an ideal president, I would take these characteristics from those I have interviewed.

Harry S Truman—feisty decisiveness, even directness.

Dwight D. Eisenhower—popularity.

John F. Kennedy—humor, grace.

Lyndon B. Johnson—power.

Richard M. Nixon—astuteness in foreign affairs.

Gerald Ford—decency.

Jimmy Carter—ethical.

Ronald Reagan—intuition.

George H. W. Bush—coalitionist.

William J. Clinton—resiliency.

George W. Bush—amiability before 9/11, ??? after the Iraq War.

Why Write a Book Anyway?

I, for one, believe I lived in the glorious era of newspapering. For the most part, editors and publishers of newspapers, particularly small to medium-sized publications, were free to be positive influences of the communities they served.

How did I get inspired to start this book? I'm glad you asked. Why would I desire to put my random thoughts and memories in book form? Let me explain.

All my life since I could read I've had a love affair with newspapers and the printed word.

An uncle of mine was editor of the Preston, Minnesota, newspaper, quite brilliant in fact until he married and bought a hotel in Denver, Colorado, at the time the Great Depression started…to his dismay.

However, even before we nephews and nieces reached our teens, we delighted in the marvelous short stories he typed and mailed to us. They lovingly were packed into a bureau drawer, human-interest material at its best. Why didn't he write a book? The hotel debacle drained him of his creative energy. What a waste of talent!

My work and my relationships as editor and publisher of daily newspapers in the Midwest gave me opportunities to explore other avenues of writing as well. If you're wondering—and probably you aren't—I inherited a weekly newspaper column when the talented State Senator Frank Johnson, a former Chautauqua speaker, died suddenly after I became editor and later publisher of the *Star-Courier* in Kewanee, Illinois. (No, he did not die because I became editor-publisher.) Frank was such a talented orator that few speakers wanted him to make their introductions, because few could measure up to his interesting remarks. Frank had written a remarkable column called the "Window Trimmer" which became "Not All Malarkey" when I inherited his space.

Therefore, this book will not be solely about presidents, but about some of the interviews I've had during the years. And about the joy I received personally from writing newspaper columns and features, not just in the four daily newspapers I served, but in a number of papers in other states where I often freelanced as a contributing writer. In addition, I'll add a few human-interest stories also that may surprise you. For example, U.S. Senator Joseph McCarthy once removed a cigar from my mouth and dunked it in my coffee. In addition, I was interviewed five times on National Public Radio because of a Nixon editorial I wrote.

Will He Write a Book?

Some of my friends (perhaps all three of them) have been guessing that someday I would write a book about the eleven U.S. presidents I have interviewed and photographed in my career as a newspaperman.

When I gave talks around the country years ago, I was inspired to write a book because of the popularity of one which was entitled *Childbirth without Fear.* I told a group that I may have written it in my column, but after the birth of our eighth child, I changed the sequel from *Childbirth Without Fear* to *Fear Without Childbirth.*

When I became publisher of the *Star-Courier* in Kewanee, Illinois, after years as an editor of the La Crosse, Wisconsin, *Tribune,* corporation officials declared that I had to meet the public and give specified talks. They even invited the president of the corporation, Philip D. Adler, so he, too, could assess what that guy (me) had to say.

The first talk was planned and Mr. Adler, a kindly gentleman, apologized because he was to be on a trip to London. Undaunted, officials sent me out on another speaking assignment and Mr. Adler again was invited, but this time he wrote that he had an engagement in New York.

Can you believe it? A third speech was scheduled, but Mr. Adler demurred, saying he had an engagement in Chicago.

Always the optimist, I figured I must be improving because he wasn't going so far to get away from me.

Therefore, without further rambling, I shall begin to describe the interviews of the last eleven presidents of the United States.

PART ONE

Presidential Interviews

Chapter One

Harry S Truman

Truman: Feisty decisiveness, even directness.

He followed probably the most powerful president, Franklin Delano Roosevelt. However, in my mind, Truman was one of the more remarkable presidents to occupy the White House.

Truman was not the first president I saw. Being a native of Wisconsin, I early knew that the state was one distinguished by its political history.

The first presidential interview I had was with Harry S Truman and it was the most historic for me. My editor in La Crosse, Wisconsin, was Roy Bangsberg of *The Tribune* and he assigned me to ride on President Truman's presidential campaign train through Minnesota and Wisconsin on October 14, 1948.

Truman's train, the Ferdinand Magellan, chugged through Minnesota and Wisconsin stopping in six towns and in the two states. I will just capture the highlights of what he said in these stops. I think the information and the way Truman spoke will convey why people voted for him in 1948.

On October 14, 1948, in Mankato, Minnesota, at 8:08 a.m. He said:

> Mankato is a good example of the close dependence of farms on cities and cities on farms in this country. Farm prosperity makes for more business in the cities, and more jobs in the great factories in your town. Similarly, when production and employ-

ment are high and workers are receiving good pay, the farmer is able to find a ready market for his products.

Last year the farmers of Minnesota made six times what they made in 1932. Now that was not by accident. It was carefully planned and carefully administered by the Democratic administrations of the last 16 years.

Thanks to the Rural Electrification Act, six out of every ten Minnesota farms has electricity, and we're going to get those other four before we get through.

However, in order to do that you've got to vote for yourselves. You've got to put somebody in the White House and in the Congress that will look after your interests.

Nine out of every ten Republicans voted against rural electrification last year. Big business is opposed to cooperatives, and the big power companies are particularly opposed to rural electrification. You see, they don't get the rake-off when the farmers' cooperatives run the electric power for the farmers. The Democratic Party supported the REA. The Democratic Party is always on the side of the people, just as you'll find the Republican Party is always on the side of special interests.

Only a third of the registered voters turned out to vote in 1946. The Republicans took over Congress as a result. They started an investigation of cooperatives in an effort to smear them. I know something about congressional investigations. I was chairman of that special committee that was formed to investigate the national defense program during the war, and I think I carried on more investigations than any other Senator in the history of the Senate over that 3-year period. Moreover, we didn't carry on smear investigations. We carried on investigations for the purpose of introducing legislation to cure ills of the country.

Do you know how you can stop this attack on cooperatives? Come out and vote on November the second, and get your friends to come out and vote. When you vote the Democratic ticket, you are not only voting for me and this good man who is running for the Senate in Minnesota, and the Congressman—you are voting for yourselves and your own interests.

You, the people, are the Government. Now, get up early on election day, go down to the polls, and vote for yourselves. And when you do that, you'll vote a straight Democratic ticket and you'll have the country in safe hands for another four years, and the President won't be obliged to be troubled by the housing problem—I can stay in the White House another four years.

We got to Waseca, Minnesota, at 9:06 a.m. He said many of these same things but here are a few differences.

I spent some time in St. Paul last night explaining what the Republican Congress had done to the people and what they have not done for the people. They don't like to hear that because they have no comeback. They can't defend the action of the Republican Congress, which is a pattern of what we're going to get unless people take an interest in their own affairs and get out and vote for their own interests. Now if you vote for your own interests here in this district, you'll send Karl Rolvaag to the Congress, and you'll send Hubert Humphrey to the Senate, and then there will be people in the Congress with whom your President can work in the public interest, for your interest.

We then stopped in Rochester, Minnesota, at 10:25 a.m. I'll just mention some different things he said here.

Thousands and thousands of Americans, distinguished Americans and plain citizens, have come to this great city to recover their health. I am on a crusade across the country to see that we don't have to send the Federal Government itself to Rochester to get it put back together after four years of Republican rule in Washington. I am here to tell you that if we have four more years like that, it will take all the clinics in the country to put it back together again.

I wish the whole nation could have the opportunity to enjoy the kind of medical care that is available here in Rochester. Last January, I asked Mr. Oscar Ewing who is the Federal Security Administrator to make a careful study of the present level of the national health. His study revealed some shocking facts. Every year, now listen to this, every year, more than 325,000 Americans die who could have been saved if they had had the right kind of medical attention and care that we know how to provide.

Only 20 percent of our population is able to afford the medical care they need. That is a disgrace to the richest country in the world. [Other facts were given] I think these facts point to the need for the national health program that I have been urging the Congress to adopt. We ought to have adequate public health services, more medical research and more medical schools, more hospitals and more doctors in nearly every area in the country, a system of insurance to cover the cost of medical care, and insurance which will protect workers against loss of earnings during illness.

The 80th Congress is a shining example of how the Republicans work. That Congress legislated absolutely for the special interests, and the people, well, I can't say the word I would like to say to what they did to the people. Don't do that again. Now, do your duty on election day. If enough of you vote, I am just as certain as I stand here that we will have a Democratic President in the White House and we will have a Democratic Congress in the 81st Congress.

We then stopped in Winona, Minnesota at 11:45 a.m. Again, I'll just mention some things Truman only said here.

I have been traveling through Minnesota since yesterday at noon. It has not only been fine to see your rich farmland, and the great grain elevators, and your cities enjoying greater prosperity than ever before in history. You know that this prosperity did not just happen. It was brought about by 16 years of control of the government by Democratic administrations. One key in the Democratic prosperity program was the Commodity Credit

Corporation. One job of the Commodity Credit Corporation was to increase grain storage facilities, so that bumper crops could be marketed over a longer period of time, thus making it unnecessary for the farmer to sell all his wheat or his corn to big speculators at very cheap prices. That is just plain robbery of the farmers.

This election will decide the future of the Commodity Credit Corporation. It will decide whether soil conservation and reforestation go forward with the Democrats, or go backwards with the Republicans. It will decide whether we have slum clearance, and low-rent housing, and good rural housing with the Democrats, or whether we shall have a housing shortage under a Republican administration. It will decide whether we will have full development of our great river system, so that cities like Winona can develop into great river ports, or whether eastern power and railroad lobbies get control under the Republicans.

This is one of the most important elections this country has faced in forty years, and it will have its effects for generations to come. Go out and vote, and I am here to tell you that if everybody in this country expresses his opinion and votes, I am not worried about the result.

The next stop was at Sparta, Wisconsin at 1:03 p.m. He said much of the same but added some personal information.

You know, in every State people have turned out just like this because I think they are interested in the welfare of the country, and they want to know what the president looks like, and what he thinks. I have been very frank in telling them just what I think—and you'll have to make up your mind as to what I look like.

You know, in years gone by, when I was a kid—21 or 22 years old—the National Guard used to come to Sparta, Wisconsin. I belonged to a battery over in Missouri. We used to come up here to do some shooting with old 3-inch guns that the artillery was then equipped with; and I had many a good time in this town in those days.

One of these programs [that started under the administration of President Roosevelt] that the people of Wisconsin know a great deal about is soil conservations. You know what conservation has meant to the American farmer. Wisconsin and Minnesota and Iowa and Missouri and Illinois were letting the farms wash away and were making counties in Louisiana. Well, we have stopped that. The Democratic soil conservation program has been extended to nearly three million farms in this country. But we ought not to rest until every acre in the country is properly managed so that it will retain its fertility permanently.

I understand you have a Republican running for Governor in this state who is running on a program of soil conservation. Can you imagine that! Don't be fooled by Republican promises. Look at the record.

Think what the Department of Agriculture is doing this year to help some of your local people here north of Sparta, your cranberry growers. Cranberry growers never received that kind of help from a single Republican administration that I know of.

Our next stop was in Elroy, Wisconsin at 1:55 p.m. That afternoon, Truman gave an address in Madison at the University of Wisconsin at 4:25 p.m. We were in Waukesha, Wisconsin by 6:46 p.m. Here are few of the differences from what he said earlier in the day.

I sincerely hope that all you young people over here on the right will be as quiet as possible so I can tell the people what I think, because when the train goes out, I'll promise to stay out here on the back platform, and every one of you will get a chance to look.

Waukesha is an industrial city in the center of a rich agricultural area. You know what I mean when I say "you're for the people." Industry, the farm, the small merchant, are all in the same boat. Their interests are all with the Democratic Party, which looks after the welfare of the people as a whole.

The real progressive movement in the nation today is in the Democratic Party. We stand for laws to bring down the cost of living, laws to insure that the farmer receives a parity income, comprehensive housing laws to clear away slums and provide decent low-rental housing, and better rural housing, a genuine national health program, better schools in both cities and rural areas, and a fair labor-management law to replace that shameful Taft-Hartley Act.

All I ask is that you look at the record. And then get your friends and your neighbors and be sure that everybody votes on the second of November.

This turned out to be a fabulous experience and adventure. I could not believe the wealth of information possessed by this man who spoke from the platform at the rear of the train. He was energetic, blunt, informed, and direct. Probably many will remember how important politics was to residents in Wisconsin and Minnesota, especially in the Badger State. The region was criss-crossed by most candidates. Of course, in the early days the La Follettes were revered.

In my youth I became interested in the La Follette dynasty with leaders of that family who became part of the state's political fabric. Phil and Bob La Follette (governor and senator of Wisconsin) were well-regarded.

As a Boy Scout in La Crosse, Wisconsin, I was invited to a La Follette rally at the First Congregational Church with instructions to stand by and offer assistance, if requested.

The speaker needed a glass of water so I was told to bring one. It was a rather embarrassing experience because as I approached the head table, I half spilled the water on the linens in front of him.

The father of Phil and Robert was "Battling Bob" La Follette, who formed the Progressive party out of the Republican. He became governor and even campaigned for president. At this late date, I am not certain of which son I tried to douse with water.

Later my father took me to the Burlington Station in La Crosse to see Al Smith, New York Democrat and 1928 presidential candidate. Later my mother drove me to Winona, Minnesota, to see Franklin Delano Roosevelt himself.

In those days because of an early primary in Wisconsin, the event attracted many campaigners, Earl Warren (later a Supreme Court judge), Estes Kefauver, Joe (Tailgunner) McCarthy, Truman, and dozens of others.

On that historic Harry Truman train excursion, all of us were assigned seats. After a while, I thought to heck with this plan, so I started down the aisle through the 16 cars, carrying a Speed Graphic camera.

As I got halfway through the last car, two Secret Service agents were sprawled there in chairs and one asked, "Where do you think you are going, Bub?"

I replied that I wanted to see the president. Just then, Truman poked his head around the corner to ask, "What's going on?" He was easy to identify with his pop bottle lenses.

So I explained I was a newspaperman with the western Wisconsin delegation and wanted to get his photo.

Truman showed me that he was truly a man of the people when he invited me to go back and get some of the delegates, adding, "And be sure to bring at least one woman."

Not surprisingly I brought two women—Mrs. Oliver Witte and Mrs. Jerry Garvin, along with Carl W. Thompson, candidate for governor.

There was always something fascinating that attracted me to Harry Truman, especially after that comment. I had three or four meetings with Truman and somehow I never got an earful of the earthy vocabulary for which he was famous. He was a captain in the artillery service during World War I and may have salted his language there. He wrote several letters to me and told me he had included my photographs of him in his Independence, Missouri, library. How could you not like this man?

There was a good reason why he became famous for his "Give 'em Hell, Harry" nickname because he constantly had to prove himself. First of all, he was woefully unprepared to be president of the United States. It's amazing that he was able to emerge from the shadow of his powerful president, Franklin Roosevelt. When he first learned that FDR hoped to name him his vice president, Truman is quoted as reacting, "Tell him to go to hell."

He was always proud to display the front page of the *Chicago Tribune* with the bold, but incorrect, headline, "DEWEY BEATS TRUMAN". I don't know if I should admit it, but when this book was nearing completion, I had Truman's photo of the *Tribune* headline modified to read, "BUY JERRY'S BOOK." I hope this advice is followed.

President Truman on October 14, 1948, with Mrs. Oliver Witte (l) and Mrs. Jerry Garvin (r), and Carl W. Thompson, candidate for governor.
Inscribed: "To Jerry Moriarity from Harry S. Truman."

**President Truman on October 14, 1948, addressing a crowd
with loud speakers.
Inscribed: "To Jerry Moriarity from Harry S Truman."**

Truman's train made two important stops in Winona, Minnesota, and Sparta, Wisconsin, with some 5,000 people jamming areas around the train at both stops. He was in a jovial mood, delighted in taking verbal jabs at Republicans, especially at Tom Dewey, who was criticized for blaming his train engineer for making a jerky stop. Truman picked up the railroaders' votes on that blast by Dewey.

There always has been a question about Truman on whether he had a middle name or just used the initial S. I thought his autographs should provide the answer to the "initial" question. However, one of the autographs on my photo had a period after the S. and the second did not. And the same with his autographed letters. One had a period after the S and the other did not.

As I understand it, Truman had two grandfathers whose first names started with S. It is said that Truman's parents could not decide on which name to use and settled for the initial. The maternal grandfather's name was Solomon and the paternal grandfather's name was Shippe. He was given no middle name, only the S. Why he wrote a period after one S and not the other remains a mystery because if S is his middle name, it needs no period. He did acknowledge displaying my photos in his museum so that was all that was important.

Truman did live in a freer era when he could leave the Mayfair Hotel in Washington, D.C., and take his daily constitutional stroll with only a few reporters and Secret Service personnel with him. Truman started his day every morning with a brisk walk at 150 paces per minute around the old neighborhood. Anybody was welcome to tag along. All they had to do was keep up. He would talk to them as if he had known them all their lives. Wouldn't it be great if presidents could do that now?

I always felt Truman was a man of the people, perky, fearless, courageous, imaginative, unpretentious and known as an uncommon man in his hometown of Independence, Missouri. I thought he got elected because he talked with the people, and I saw him do it, whereas I think Thomas Dewey talked to the people.

He brought World War II to a close by dropping an atomic bomb twice on Japan, although he did not know such a bomb existed until he became president. As a radar navigator on B-29s when the war ended, I was grateful Truman dropped those bombs because we had spent months studying Japan and eventually we were slated for aerial duty over Japan. I will never forget the conversation that Truman had with Paul Tibbets who dropped the A-bomb from his *Enola Gay* plane. The newsmen reported that Tibbets said, "He told me I had done my duty and that if anyone criticized me for dropping the bomb, I should send that person to see him because he gave me the order to do so."

My wife and I saw how great the devastation was when we visited Hiroshima and Nagasaki in 2000. During our visit, Japanese propagandists still condemned the U.S. without ever acknowledging that Japan started the war by bombing Pearl Harbor.

But Truman did embroil the country in the Korean War, and fired headstrong General MacArthur who started an expansive Asian invasion policy using Taiwan troops and possibly nuclear weapons without permission. Truman made history as a remarkable president despite his colorful language, his Pendergast ties and his fondness for buttermilk laced with bourbon. However, little mention is made about how Truman rebuffed Ho Chi Minh who asked for assistance after France lost its colonial power in the Far East. The Vietnamese letter requesting assistance from the U.S. against the French was dated February 16, 1945, and was never answered.

When Truman died in 1972, I wrote a story called "Some Memories of Truman" on December 27, 1972.

Some Memories of Truman

What a gutty fighter to the last.

Somehow, we knew the Lord Himself had to come down through the clouds to drag him to the heavens or, at the very least, to some limbo where retired presidents can rest through eternity.

In our mind's eye, we visualized that scrappy Harry had literally to be carried off this globe, much as Sewell Avery, doughty Montgomery Ward head, had to be carried off by marshals, who hoisted him in his chair and dumped him out of his office.

Avery, the business tycoon, and Truman, the Missouri politician, were anachronisms of three-score years ago, but neither would give up without a fight.

Harry Truman dead? We can't believe it!

We had our first personal introduction to President Truman way back on Thursday, October 14, 1948. Roy L. Bangsberg, then editor of the *La Crosse Tribune,* where I was laboring as state editor in those postwar years, asked if I would like to try my hand at political writing.

The assignment? Riding on Truman's presidential campaign train through Minnesota and Wisconsin.

Although I barely knew the back end of a camera from the front, I was handed a bulky Speed Graphic, several holders of 4 x 5 film, and a couple of sleeves of large bulbs. It wasn't easy being a photographer in those pre-Instamatic days.

I was put aboard a special 16-car train at Winona, Minnesota, and naively set about hunting for the president.

As I reached the final car, two Secret Service men blocked my way, asked, "Where do you think you're going, Bub?"

"To see Truman," came my feeble reply. Just then Truman—the Man himself—poked his head around the corner to learn what was going on.

And he sympathetically interceded when I said I wanted a picture of him and part of the western Wisconsin delegation. He even suggested I get a woman for the photo. I did him even better, getting two women. The group included Carl Thompson of Stoughton, candidate for governor, and two Elroy women, Mrs. Oliver Witte and Mrs. Jerry Garvin.

High point of the journey was the whistle-stop appearance in Sparta, Wisconsin. Truman made capital with the railroaders when he defended the railroad's engineer.

Looking fit and happy, Truman had a good-natured pat on the back for his engineer, but he offered nothing but criticism for the Republicans before a crowd of 5,000 at the Sparta Northwestern Railroad Depot early that October afternoon.

Truman concentrated on the soil conservation and rural electrification administration planks in his party platform in his folksy address from the rear platform.

The President laughed heartily when someone in the audience asked him, "How are you and your engineer getting along?" recalling the name-calling episode of Republic candidate Thomas Dewey. In a pique, Dewey tacked the term "lunatic" on his engineer when he backed into a crowd during one of Dewey's talks.

"The engineer and I are getting along all right," Truman said, quickly adding, "He hasn't jarred us a bit today. But, most of the engineers and farmers are Democrats anyway."

The crowd, which included many children, cheered when Truman confided with a smile, "They know what side their bread is buttered on."

He followed this with a loud stage whisper, "And if you know what side your bread is buttered on, you'll vote for me, too." Apparently, they did.

Truman said he remembered Sparta and nearby Camp McCoy. He had trained there with a field artillery unit of the Missouri National Guard during the First World War, rising to the rank of captain.

Master of ceremonies for the Sparta visit was John D. Rice, Sparta newsman and candidate for the state assembly.

Truman recognized Laverne Hall of Westby, a member of the Coon Prairie 4-H Club, who a year earlier had been selected as the outstanding 4-H youth in the nation. Hall had a 25-minute conference with Truman in 1947 after winning national honors.

The two Tomah girls who presented Truman with cranberries were Jacqueline Thouveneil and Marise Grovesteen.

At the conclusion of his talk, Truman introduced his wife and daughter, Margaret, and they drew heavy applause.

Mrs. Truman looked like a proud wife during her husband's speech, although sometimes she appeared to be worrying about his new haircut (or lack of it) or the press of his trousers. Wives worried about that in those days. This time I knew how to use a camera and took many pictures of Truman surrounded by dignitaries of politics, stage, and screen.

Harry Truman with Bess (l.) and Margaret (r.) Harry and Margaret's seeming coifs are thanks to people behind them.

Back in the late 1970s, I made copies, sent them to Truman in Independence, and he personally autographed several for me. He even added a thoughtful postscript, "I hope everything is going well with you and that it will continue to go that way."

He was that kind of a man to the end, a Missouri giant who inherited the Roosevelt dynasty and led this nation through a successful termination of World War II and troubled crises later.

The Lord should have left him here for us; there are so few of his type around.

Even though I had 19 presidential interviews starting with Harry Truman, almost all stuck in my throat as I rose to ask a question.

When you say, "Mr. President," and he nods in your direction, suddenly the floor is all yours. With the bright lights, you're semiconsciously aware of the banks of television cameras from the major networks in the background. After all, this is in the East Room of the White House and the press and the world, ultimately, are straining for every significant bit.

You'd like to come off sounding like an Edward R. Murrow or a Walter Cronkite, but there is an inner suspicion that a Tim Conway or even Foster Brooks may emerge from the image your voice is projecting. But the tongue-in-cheek question about newspapers and the President's daughter goes over reasonably well and, fortunately, the President responds with good humor as laughter erupts on two occasions during his reply.

Somehow, the members of the family didn't have to pretend they weren't with me, tribute enough, I'd say.

And the newspapers received a plug they can use as a promotion during National Newspaper Weeks in October. We have to grab for those tributes with all the gusto we can.

I did get to see him later at a Perle Mesta party in Chicago. I backed (yes, backed) into a Perle Mesta reception held for him and presidential candidate Adlai Stevenson.

Harry Truman enjoying an ovation.
Perle Mesta Party in Chicago

When I became editor and publisher of the Kewanee, Illinois, *Star-Courier,* I enjoyed a trip to the Democratic convention in Chicago when Adlai Stevenson was campaigning for the presidency.

Somehow, I heard that Perle Mesta, "the hostess with the mostest," was to sponsor a huge celebration at the Blackstone Hotel with

Harry Truman and other Democrat notables in attendance. That aroused my interest.

I learned that Perle Mesta had a hotel suite in the hotel across from mine so I tracked down the room number and headed there to see if I could get an invitation.

She and her secretary both came to the door and I explained, after identifying myself as a newspaperman from the Lee Enterprises Corporation, that I would like an invitation to that night's party.

I addressed all my questions to Perle, but she deflected them, each time telling her secretary what to say, such as repeatedly saying, "Tell him we don't have any invitations left" or "Tell him it is out of the question."

Finally, I talked directly to the secretary, who had the look of an Irish lady, and I said, "Can't you do something for this Irishman?" Therefore, I wrote out my name and the hotel address and said she could contact me there.

Well, I went to the convention at the stockyards' convention center until about 5 p.m., and returned to the hotel to check my mail. There was no invitation, only a letter from the newspaper.

Nonetheless, I went to the hotel, which by then had a packed lobby. Everyone crowded near the stairway to the mezzanine, where the gala was to be. So I took an elevator to the second floor and walked down to the mezzanine, taking up a position behind the table where the secretary was checking off the guest list.

So I remained there to snap pictures of the prominent guests from the political and entertainment world.

When a lull developed before Adlai Stevenson, the next presidential candidate, arrived, I paused to talk to the secretary. She looked at me and snarled, "You…I tried to reach you at your hotel, but they didn't have a Jerry Moriarity registered and also didn't have a seventeenth floor." I gasped as I apparently had given her the name of the wrong hotel.

To prove I wasn't an imposter, I pulled out the letter received just that afternoon from my newspaper with my name and hotel correctly listed.

Sadly, I heard her say, "Well, I tried, but that's the best I could do." What a bummer.

However, I hadn't lost hope because Stevenson had not yet arrived. And when he did, there was so much activity around him I kept snapping pictures and backed into the room.

Once inside, I was able to take a variety of photos. Another fellow was standing near me, so we started talking. He asked if I had an invitation and I said no, that I had backed into the room. "How about you?" I asked, and he replied that he didn't either. I asked, "Well, how did you get in?" And he said, "I came in through the kitchen." It turned out he was a steel salesman from Chicago.

Then the first of the attractive waitresses came in with champagne glasses with pink ribbons tied around the stems. Before long, we had at least eight glasses on a nearby partition.

After a great social period, Perle and some official stood nearby and she whispered to give the press another two minutes and then clear the room.

With that signal, I was where two Secret Service agents were standing, so I put my camera down by the wall next to one of them and took off my press credentials.

When the lovely meal was served, this salesman and I could have been first and second in the line, but we let some woman have that honor. Gracious of us, wasn't it?

One of the esteemed reporters of the *Chicago Daily News* wrote the next day that he stared into the room after being expelled and finally went down the street to have pizza.

The salesman and I didn't have that problem as we enjoyed the fruits of Perle Mesta's labors.

By the way, I did receive a nice letter from the secretary several days later, saying she had a hunch I got into the party on my own.

As long as I wrote some rather favorable comments about Harry Truman, he probably would not have minded that I misappropriated his famous headline from the *Chicago Daily Tribune* to promote sales for this book. The original banner headline prematurely proclaimed that the New York Republican, Thomas Dewey, had defeated Truman. We're sure, too, that Dewey would not mind being left out of the headline reproduction. It took a while for the *Chicago Tribune* to live down the error and even a longer time for Truman to end his gloating.

November 3, 1948, Harry Truman found "Dewey Beats Truman" in the *Chicago Daily Tribune*.

My little joke was a take-off of the famous line in this newspaper:

**Truman's famous newspaper joke. I hope
he would have liked this headline.**

I have often said he never could be elected president in this era with his pop bottle lenses, his rather raspy voice and high school education. Harry S Truman (May 8, 1884-December 26, 1972) was the 33rd president, from 1945-53, and served with Vice President Alben Barkley.

Chapter Two

Dwight David Eisenhower

Eisenhower—Popularity and Activism

Dwight D. Eisenhower, a man of dignity, gave America the breather it needed after World War II when he was probably the most popular man in the world. His worldwide popularity undoubtedly would be his greatest ranking attribute. In one of his many worldwide appearances after the war, in India alone crowds of well over a million mobbed him.

Eisenhower was criticized in the press during the terms of his office as president for not doing enough, but liberals and neo-conservatives have rediscovered his attributes as an activist.

Not to be overlooked were his civil rights legislation in the wake of the Little Rock, Arkansas, unrest, and the greatest construction project in the history of the modern world. The four-lane, coast-to-coast, border-to-border interstate highway project was an even greater construction project than the Great Wall of China.

As an aviation cadet and then an Air Force officer in World War II, I and most of us in the service recognized Eisenhower as a hero for his leadership in Europe as Supreme Commander.

I probably had less personal contact with Dwight Eisenhower than any other president except Lyndon Johnson, but my dislike for Johnson caused that.

I first met Eisenhower when he and Richard Nixon arrived at the Chicago airport on July 5, 1952, for the Republican National Convention. He appeared that night at the Chicago Blackstone Theater for an Eisenhower Rally.

Three of us from the press were invited to a special room to meet Eisenhower and his wife, Mamie, and Nixon and his wife, Pat. It was a strange gathering. The four dignitaries were seated on a davenport, but we were told just to take photographs and not question them. It made no sense at all.

Eisenhower looked great, as usual, with his 360-degree smile. At the time, I thought how could anyone dislike this commander of Allied forces who was now the leader of the free world?

In contrast to Eisenhower, Nixon sat on the opposite side of the davenport and he looked glum and impassive. This was after he was put through the meat grinder to prove he was competent to be veep or as Eisenhower said, "To be as clean as a hound dog's tooth." Later Nixon had to rely on his "Checkers speech" to stay in the good graces of Ike.

I still have my photo of the four sitting on a davenport at the Chicago airport in 1952 with Nixon looking young and quite apprehensive, in my view. Nixon's "Checker's speech" was two months later on September 23, 1952.

**Presidential candidate Dwight Eisenhower and Mamie with
vice-presidential candidate Richard Nixon and Pat in 1952.**

The Republican Convention was held in the Chicago Convention Center from July 7 to 10th and besides Presidential nominees Eisenhower, Robert Taft (son of President William Howard Taft), and undeclared candidate General Douglas MacArthur. Eisenhower received the nomination for President on July 11, 1952. In his acceptance speech, Ike told convention delegates that they had called him to lead a great campaign. He described it as a campaign for freedom in America and for freedom in the world. He chose Senator Richard Nixon of California as his vice presidential candidate. By that time, Nixon was known throughout the United States for his strong opposition to communism and he could also bring in the state of California with its large electoral vote.

This was the first televised national convention. Wary of the political damage that could be caused by cameras, delegates were told not to look tired or to fall asleep during their candidate's speech.

Oh, yes, here is a photo I like. At the Chicago Republican convention, I took a close-up of a black (now African American) delegate and Eisenhower, deep in thoughtful conversation. The two bore studied appearances, their expressions and facial features quite similar to one another.

**President Eisenhower and African American delegate
at Chicago Republican Convention in 1952.**

This convention was only one month before Eisenhower's famous "I shall go to Korea" speech on October 25, 1952. The country was upset with Truman and Democrats over the war in Korea, which killed so many troops. Eisenhower pledged:

> Now, where will a new administration begin. It will begin with its president taking a firm, simple resolution. That resolution will be to forego the diversions of politics and to concentrate on the job of ending the Korean War, until that job is honorably done. That job requires a personal trip to Korea. Only in that way could I learn how best to serve the American people in the cause of peace. I shall go to Korea.

That same year, one of the worst enemies of President Eisenhower was Senator Joseph McCarthy, who was making more of Communists than Ike thought he should. Eisenhower's opponent, Democrat Adlai Stevenson had already criticized Sen. McCarthy several times.

However, Eisenhower held his peace, even when McCarthy accused his top WWII General. On June 14, 1951, Sen. McCarthy said that then Secretary of Defense George Marshall "aided the Communist drive for world domination" and implied that he was a traitor to his country. Decent Eisenhower hated these words, which drove Marshall into retirement, but Ike said nothing publicly.

Of all the photos of Eisenhower I took, two are memorable for me. He went to Peoria, Illinois, to give a major farm policy speech to farm leaders at which the press was excluded. Not able to get in, I wandered around the building, apparently as his meeting was about to end. A doorkeeper, who recognized me, beckoned me with a wave of his fingers and opened the door quickly so I could enter. He held a finger to his lips as he motioned me inside. People like that are invaluable.

And what a surprise! The leading national and state politicians were walking toward the exit when they spotted me. They all have startled looks at this breach of security. My photo shows U.S. Rep. Leslie Ahrends, who points to me as the miscreant, and behind him is Gov. William Stratton of Illinois who looks angrier than the rest. Next to President Eisenhower is the eloquent Senator Everett Dirksen, looking a little lost for words.

**Congressman Leslie Ahrends (l), Gov. William
Stratton, President Eisenhower and U.S.
Sen. Everett Dirksen discovering me.**

Needless to say I beat a hasty exit, but outside was confronted by a television reporter with a camera focused on me. He wanted to know what went on and somehow I muttered that they were discussing farm parities, of which I knew little. However, that was my first appearance on live television.

President Eisenhower and his wife chat with Sen. Everett Dirksen in Peoria, Illinois, on September 26, 1956.

I did get a banner headline September 26, 1956, on Eisenhower's speech the night before in which he assailed Adlai Stevenson's farm plans. He derided Adlai's rigid price controls as a "mockery and deceit," when addressing a crowd of 10,000 cheering Republicans. He delivered his talk at Bradley University field house to an overflow crowd. His wife also was there to share in the applause. Here are a few quotations from his speech that night.

Rigidly fixing price supports at 90 percent of parity without regard to supply conditions--and so encouraging surpluses that depress market prices--is for the farmer, mockery and deceit. That kind of program compels drastic quotas, allotments, government regulation. It is a program for politicians, not for farmers.

Today farm foreclosures are near an all-time low. Today more farm operators own their farms than ever before. Today the value of farm lands is at an all-time high. Today farm income is at a billion dollar rate above last year. And the long decline in farm prices has stopped.

Prices today are higher than last April when I vetoed the hodge-podge that the politicians called a farm bill. Prices are 7 per cent higher than last December. They are higher than a year ago when high rigid price supports still applied to the so-called basic crops. This, of course, is no final solution. But, I repeat, this is a good start in the right direction.

Tonight I have talked mainly of farming. But I realize that other things mean at least as much to you and to your family. I remind you of the contrast between today and the life we knew, and the government we knew, four years ago in foreign policy and in farm policy, in military affairs and in fiscal affairs, in states' rights and in civil rights, in tax policy and in labor policy. Where there was confusion then, today there is sense and order. Where there was doubt, there is confidence. My friends, I believe that these facts plainly mark the path of our nation's progress.

Whatever you believe, my fellow citizens, you know what your personal role in this coming decision must be: To register, to get all your friends to register, to vote, to get all your friends to vote, so that on November 6th your voices, the voices of all of you, will be heard.

Somehow through Eisenhower's presidential terms I probably took more photos of him than the other presidents, although it would be close to the number of John F. Kennedy photos.

When Eisenhower died, I lamented the fact that despite all the photos I took of him, I never requested an autograph. That prompted me to send duplicates of pictures to other presidents with the hope of attracting their autographs.

Dwight D. Eisenhower (October 14, 1890-March 28, 1969) was the 34th president, serving from 1953-61 with Vice President Richard Nixon.

Chapter Three

John Fitzgerald Kennedy

Kennedy—Humor and grace.

John F. Kennedy, the youngest (41) ever elected president (Theodore Roosevelt was youngest to serve) and the youngest to die (11-22-63), possessed charm, youth and vigor.

Our 35th president could have been a movie star, or almost anything he desired with his charm, humor, handsome appearance and, of, yes, plenty of money. But he wanted to be president—or at least his father wanted him to be president as second choice. John's older brother, Joe, Jr., was supposed to be the candidate for high office, but he was killed in World War II as a combat pilot, so the honor fell to John.

Not only was he gorgeous to look at, as most women admitted, he was blessed with charm and a marvelous sense of humor. Kennedy proved to be an inspirational, although somewhat ineffective, leader with an ability to laugh at himself. Charisma, an overused Greek word, seemed to have been invented solely for him.

It was interesting that John Kennedy and Richard Nixon both were elected to Congress at the same time. John's father, in fact, liked Nixon and offered to help him financially. And it was somewhat ironic that Kennedy and Nixon campaigned at the same time for president. Kennedy became the first Catholic ever elected to the high office by beating Nixon in one of the closest elections in political history. When Kennedy succeeded Eisenhower, I overheard some of the Kennedy electees say they were admonished not to make harsh comments about the elderly Eisenhower backers because the Kennedy supporters were so young in contrast. Nice approach!

When I first saw him at a Democratic National Convention in Chicago, I predicted great things for him in national politics. This I did in the first news article I sent back to the Kewanee, Illinois, *Star-Courier,* where I had just been named editor. Senator John Kennedy surprised the 1956 Democratic National Convention in Chicago by a nomination speech so good that he quickly became a contender for Stevenson's vice-presidential running mate. The notes of this speech have been found and this is one of the last speeches Kennedy ever wrote himself. He met Ted Sorenson (speech writer and research-er/editor for *Profiles in Courage*) in 1956. Here is the conclusion of Kennedy's speech:

> These are critical times—times that demand the best we have—times that demand the best America has. Fellow dele-gates, I give you the man from Libertyville—the next Demo-cratic nominee and the next President of the United States—Adlai E. Stevenson.

There was some speculation that Sen. Kennedy would be picked by Adlai Stevenson as his candidate for vice-president when Adlai ran against Eisenhower. However, Carey Estes Kefauver was a name already on most people's lips because he gained national attention as the general chairman of the Special Commission on Organized Crime in Interstate Commerce. His hearings were well televised.

I saw Adlai Stevenson many times at the convention, and recall the picture of him in which one shoe had a well-worn bare spot as an appeal to the needier voters. For years, I had one of his stick pins of a shoe with the worn bare spot, his campaign symbol. One of the frequent visitors to backstage and the convention center was Eleanor Roosevelt, widow of Franklin, as she backed the candidacy of Stevenson. I don't remember how it happened, but I spent a lot of time backstage with the politicians. Maybe it was because I carried a heavy press camera and they thought I belonged.

I learned only in recent years that Kennedy was so hurt by Stevenson's selection of Kefauver for vice president that he immediately flew to his father's French villa for pleasure yachting. He left his wife, Jackie, eight months pregnant, but returned when Jackie was near death after delivering a stillborn child.

The first time I actually met John Kennedy, he was stumping for the presidency with his sister, Eunice Shriver on October 27, 1959. He met with a Bureau County group and labor leaders at the Pere Marquette Hotel in Peoria, Illinois. It proved an interesting gathering with discussions about Richard Nixon, Kennedy's Catholic religion, and his own hopes for being elected president.

At that time, separate meetings were held for men and women. My thought was that I always could attend the men's sessions so I followed Kennedy into his women's meeting. Not only did he possess attractive looks, he charmed the women's gathering with his Irish wit. All I could note was that the women were in ecstasy. It was obvious that "the tall handsome senator with the tousled hair, flashing a smile and Boston accent" attracted a capacity crowd of 500 to this event. I quoted one woman as murmuring, "I'll vote for him regardless of what his political party is. He's beautiful."

One reporter asked him about Nixon's strength among the Republicans. He told us, "Today he's the strongest, but, of course, you won't know how strong he'll be next July."

He also believed that Nixon would be a stronger candidate than Nelson Rockefeller, which proved to be true.

Kennedy called himself the "most active among the actives" of possible candidates of his party. Most significantly he said he would declare his intentions (about running) in January.

Also in his conversation, he lamented the fact that the United States had lagged in space efforts, adding, "I don't think we spent enough or early enough." He later vindicated the U.S. effort by landing a man on the moon when he was president.

On his pulse-feeling tour of Illinois, Kennedy said he felt he was doing well and he reasserted his belief that being a Catholic would not bar a candidate from becoming president.

The most interesting part for me came later. I was standing in the doorway when he came out of the meeting room and he looked somewhat desperately at me and asked if I knew where the restroom was. I said "yes" and I would direct him if he would answer a question for me. So we chatted as I led him down the corridor. I knew he would be beyond disliking because he was so, well, charismatic (that word again).

As he came out of the restroom he smiled at me and asked, "Well, what is your question?"

Few ever considered me to be predictable, so I have to explain my strange question. It's almost shameful as I think about it because you have to go back in years to the time when publications, such as *Confidential* magazine, always featured articles saying "What is Jimmy Hoffa really like?" or "What is Cary Grant really like?"

So when he insisted, I paused before asking, "What is Peter Lawford really like?" Peter, a movie star, was Kennedy's brother-in-law, having married his sister, Patricia. I started to break into a broad grin and so did he as he slapped me on the back.

Somehow, this got the two of us off to a great start. A newsman, Ralph Benton, from Princeton, Illinois, saw us at that joyous moment and snapped a picture, which caught both of us in a fine mood. Kennedy never gave an educated guess to my unexpected question, except for mumbling something like, "Okay, I guess." And I can't even remember what other questions I asked.

**President John F. Kennedy and me at the Pere Marquette Hotel
in Peoria, Illinois, when I asked him about Peter Lawford.**

I also met Kennedy later at a regional meeting and was almost
shocked to see how skinny he became because of the ravages of Addison's disease, which wasn't revealed until much later.

Senator John Kennedy campaigning for the Presidency in late 1959 in Illinois showing a noticeable weight loss.

After Kennedy was elected president, I was in Washington, D.C., in the then new State Department office building on the exact day (March 9, 1962) that Kennedy confessed to us that American pilots were flying combat missions in Vietnam for the first time. Under Eisenhower, we had only an advisory role or mission. Pilots on those first combat missions started a parade of dead that seemed interminable. At Kennedy's press conference, he added that sending combat troops would be "a basic change…which calls for a constitutional decision, [and] of course I would go to the Congress."

Also, we had an ill-conceived, ill-fated Bay of Pigs invasion of Cuba when no American air power was provided to the men who were invading Cuba to free that island from Castro's grip. President Kennedy stunned everyone but gained accolades when he publicly took blame for the decision to launch the invasion. He noted, however, that intelligence had given him information that was inaccurate and asked for changes in the Central Intelligence Agency.

It was interesting to note also that when his advisers asked Kennedy to start an economic blockade of Cuba, he had to give up smoking Cuban cigars, which he had come to enjoy since his marriage. He delayed long enough so he could have Cuban cigars shipped to him. However, his last Cuban cigars were a gift of 150 from Nikita Khrushchev who had received them from Fidel Castro.

Jackie had encouraged her husband to smoke so that he would not object to her smoking. [The public never knew that Jackie smoked until the day of the assassination when she smoked while waiting for doctors to finish examining Kennedy at Parkland Hospital.]. Despite these rather negative comments, I became a great fan of Kennedy.

My last visit to the White House during Kennedy's administration was in 1963 and I had the special treat of watching and listening to Pierre Salinger play the piano.

President Kennedy's press secretary played an impromptu concert after making several announcements. Salinger, a piano child prodigy, also served as President Johnson's press secretary. He then moved to Paris and later London until his death in 2004.

**President Kennedy's press secretary, Pierre
Salinger, playing the piano.**

I teased Pierre Salinger with a Flat Stanley cutout. This was the
rage of second graders a few years ago. The second graders of Rock
Island, Illinois, were thrilled to learn that Flat Stanley had met many
Washington, D.C., dignitaries.

**Flat Stanley met Pierre Salinger to the
delight of many second graders.**

Jerry Moriarity, the author, at the White House in 1963.

I did write many stories about Kennedy after other meetings with him. And I admire how he could handle tough critics in the news corps, such as Helen Thomas. He could twist their questions around and leave most everyone laughing. But I must admit that his light-heartedness suggested that he might not take some things seriously enough. We know now that he began the Viet Nam War but I don't believe he understood how many Americans might be killed or wounded in that war. I also believe that he did not want it to become an all-consuming American war and wanted to gradually bring the troops back home.

However, I think his mind was on lighter things, women or conquests, making a good impression, enjoying the pomp of his position, and I doubt that he thought deeply about things such as that. But he was delightful.

I will add that in my contacts with him, I noted a tremendous change in his physical appearance. My earlier views of him were as a skinny but handsome young man, who seemed a little fatigued. My last view of him was quite different, energetic, less handsome with cheeks that had filled out with some fat, tall with a rather stiff back and a very slight hump at the back of his neck. He looked as if he had been in the sun a lot, something a president rarely has time to do.

I did not know that he was probably wearing the back brace that he wore at the time of his death, causing the stiffness. Nor did the public learn for some years that he and his brother had lied about John having Addison's disease.

After his assassination, the autopsy showed that his adrenal cortices, which lie on the kidneys and supply us with hormones during times of stress, were completely gone. He had been receiving hydrocortisone, a life-threatening yet live-saving hormone which made him extremely peppy and horny, giving him the slight buffalo hump of the neck, a tan which is really a discoloration of the skin, and much thicker hair than a man of his age usually has. Those medical symptoms and the life-threatening nature of Addison's disease would have cost him the presidency, had the public known. Even a skin cancer on John McCain's face during the 2008 presidential campaign attracts alarm and attention.

Still and all, the tragedy of his assassination cut short his presidency which was largely ineffective, and shattered his potential promise. It was also not generally known that his successor, Lyndon Johnson, had suffered a near fatal heart attack in 1955, and gave up smoking until he was no longer president. If his medical condition were known, there would have been a great deal made of it by the public, reporters, and physicians.

A decade after Kennedy's assassination, I wrote this story about him for the *Ottumwa Courier* in Iowa on November 22, 1973.

Kennedy—A Fresh Hope for a Tired World

A decade ago, a stunned and saddened nation went into mourning because of the tragic assassination of President John Fitzpatrick Kennedy.

Undoubtedly, as Americans discover that the anniversary of his death falls on this Thanksgiving Day, their holiday spirits likewise will be dampened. He was a remarkable refreshing personality, a fresh hope for a tired world.

While we bow our heads in prayer over bountiful feasts today, hopefully some will reflect on how cruelly we treat our leaders. Since Kennedy's chilling murder, a second president, Lyndon B. Johnson was humbled over the agony of war and went to his death a beaten man, and today Richard M. Nixon stumbles about in a trauma of suspicion, warily trying to ward off attacks from all directions.

But today our thoughts go back to John F. Kennedy—the one who invented charisma even before the word was coined in its modern-day sense.

Tousled of hair, quick of Irish wit was he. While not of humble birth by any means, this rich man's son nonetheless had a magnetism that nourished hope in the poor and inspired promise among those who society had forgotten. And the ex citing world he was creating stood still the instant bullets began pouring into his body that fateful day in Dallas, Texas, November 22, 1963.

At the time of our first meeting, Kennedy, a U.S. senator, was a somewhat scrawny, ambitious politician attending a Democratic convention in Chicago.

Now from the standpoint of historic perspective, we're happy to recall that one of our first dispatches from Chicago focused on our belief that the Massachusetts senator would be a strong candidate for the vice presidential nod.

Our first glimpse of Kennedy occurred at a packed reception given Sunday, August 12, 1956, for Adlai Stevenson and Mrs. Franklin Roosevelt. At that time, Adlai virtually had the nomination for president sewed up except that perky Harry Truman was making waves on behalf of Averill Harriman.

But the Democrats did not "crave Ave" and Adlai was nominated. That's where Kennedy burst upon the national scene. Estes Kefauver, the lanky Tennessean of coon hat fame, was expected to be Adlai's choice. Kennedy, however, narrated a documentary that brought the convention delegates to their feet. A VP boom on behalf of Kennedy was launched and he almost won. Almost. Camelot's time had not yet come.

It was probably just as well because JFK at 39 needed a little seasoning and Dwight Eisenhower was destined for office. Both incidentally were *bonafide* heroes. We did manage to take a lot of pictures of Kennedy, however, impressed as we were with his future.

Our second meeting came in October 1959 when Kennedy was on a pulse-taking tour of the Midwest before running for president.

Normally, Kennedy was surrounded by a great number of fans. But he had checked out of a luncheon meeting in the Pere Marquette Hotel in Peoria to look for a, shhh, restroom. The lobby was almost deserted as the others were trying to get the best seats.

He had just come out of a meeting with women, where I had elected to hear him, and as he exited he asked me if I knew where the restroom was. I said I'd show him if he's answer a question for me. We chatted as we walked down the corridor. As we came face to face again, I tossed out a mildly irreverent question about his movie-star brother-in-law, asking, "What is Peter Lawford really like?"

Kennedy studied me carefully for a second and then we both broke out laughing. Somewhere along the line he mumbled in the marvelous Harvard accent, "All right, I guess." He also clapped me on the back as he laughed.

But it set the mood for a dandy interview and he posed several times for photos. When his sister, Mrs. Eunice Shriver, happened by, she also posed, both flashing those white Kennedy teeth for which the family is justly famous.

For the Peoria trip, we had stuffed some photos taken three years earlier of Kennedy in Chicago and he autographed several. And after he was president, he signed a copy of the photograph taken of both of us in the lobby by Ralph Benton of the *Rock Island Argus*. It's a treasured memento now.

The most meaningful meeting with Kennedy took place in March 1962 in Washington DC at a three-day conference with top level administration officials. The president talked candidly for 35 minutes. Ground rules were that data could be published, but not attributed to individuals. That's how the game was played then.

However, we still have our original notes on Kennedy's talk. His comments on Cuba were interesting and I can reveal them now. Describing Castro's influence in Latin America as noticeably less, JFK said, "I wouldn't be surprised if he fell apart."

Kennedy was not infallible, obviously.

In retrospect, the most chilling part of his talk concerned South Vietnam and Laos.

He made a promise of eventual victory in South Vietnam. But he sent a modest shiver through the audience with the announcement, "The United States today is acknowledging the use of American fighter pilots." The full impact, however, would not be realized until months and years later. (Prior to that time under Eisenhower, Americans had only a neutral status.)

There was a final ceremony, involving a representative of a national radio broadcasters association and Kennedy was a quick man with a phrase.

He thanked the radio man for a silver cup, but he laughingly added, "It doesn't quite measure up to what Jackie has been getting." Of course he was referring to the many lavish gifts she had been receiving as a result of her tour of India and Pakistan.

The president received a jibe from the radio man making the presentation with the latter claiming Mr. Kennedy had stated he had a preference for newspapers.

This was gracefully fielded when Kennedy replied, "This must have happened when I was inexperienced." It brought a big laugh but it also scored on a newsman who had referred to the president's inexperience in the early days of his administration during a question and answer period.

Yes, we will be remembering on this Thanksgiving Day the Kennedy era and we'll remember the happy days.

John Kennedy (May 29, 1917-November 22, 1963) was our 35th president and served from 1961-63 with Vice President Lyndon Johnson.

Chapter Four

Lyndon Baines Johnson

Johnson: Power

Johnson did what John F. Kennedy could not do, enacting the Great Society legislation. But he knew power like a salmon knows how to swim upstream—the appropriate quote from George Reedy, Marquette University professor and one-time press secretary for Johnson.

Critics said Johnson wasn't born in a log cabin, but in a manger and wanted to be buried in a shallow grave as he would be up in three days.

Of all the presidents I have interviewed, I have reacted more negatively to Lyndon B. Johnson. I had just one interview with him and that was enough. In my mind, he was a dangerous egotistical hypocrite, but he did know how to wield power, getting most of his Great Society legislation through Congress.

Johnson once said, "I'm president of the United States and I can do any goddam thing I want." And he did.

After condemning Barry Goldwater as a warmonger and proclaiming himself a disciple of peace, he got us further into war, the Vietnam debacle, unlike any other war in our history.

You're right. I am being harsh on Lyndon Johnson.

But I felt that way ever since Johnson promoted a television commercial of a small girl holding flowers, saying she would be blown up in an atomic bomb explosion if Barry Goldwater were elected president.

There is no doubt, however, that Johnson was an imposing figure. And he could pressure legislators of both parties to do his bidding. That is why I have credited Johnson's greatest attribute as POW-ER.

The first time I saw Lyndon Johnson he was standing upright on the back seat of a convertible waiting for his aides to help him down.

**President Lyndon Johnson in Peoria, Illinois,
October 7, 1964; Secret Service agent Rufus
Youngblood directed the president to dismount.**

Eventually several of his Secret Service agents came to his rescue, hoisted him in the air, and plunked him down on the lawn. It was a strange sight as most people would just sit down, open the back door, and exit the vehicle. The 36th president assumed help would be provided. I photographed him in the flying act.

He did autograph several of my pictures. I was glad to have captured a shot of the Secret Service agent, Rufus Youngblood, the partially balding man, who had protected him from Oswald's bullets in Dallas.

**President Lyndon Johnson in Peoria, Illinois,
dismounting with Secret Service aid.**

I also observed a most unusual habit in speaking to men. He walked up too close to their face, much closer than I would have been comfortable with, and stared down at them from his imposing height. In fact, that might have been one of his methods of intimidating people and forcing them to retreat, obey, or cowtow to him. And, could I be mistaken, I think I saw him even kiss one older politician on his forehead. Yes, I must have seen it because another photographer actually got a picture of him doing just that a short time later.

I covered Johnson's appearance on Wednesday, October 7, 1964, in Peoria, Illinois. It was estimated that over 25,000 jammed the streets around the Peoria County Courthouse Square. These photos were taken as he cajoled his supporters to elect him by an overwhelming margin.

President Lyndon Johnson, Peoria, Illinois, in 1964.

Here are some excerpts from his speech to the Illinois State Federation of Labor on October 7, 1964, in Peoria directing people to vote for him on November 3, 1964.

I am proud to be a Democrat. I am proud to be a member of the party of Jefferson and Jackson and Cleveland and Wilson, Franklin D. Roosevelt, Harry S. Truman. I am especially proud to be a member of the party of that great and that gallant American, John Fitzgerald Kennedy.

But I am prouder that over a career of more than 30 years in public life, I have always been the kind of Democrat who could and would work together with my fellow Americans of the party of Lincoln and McKinley, Herbert Hoover and Dwight Eisenhower, Robert Taft, Arthur Vandenberg, and Everett Dirksen.

On this bright autumn afternoon, I remember—and I know you have not forgotten—another day such as this on November 22d, we were happy and smiling and all seemed secure. Then in one terrible, incredible instant our world and our times changed. A vicious bullet from an assassin had felled a noble man.

Wherever we were, whatever we were doing, Americans laid down their own interests and had only one thought: their nation's interest.

I said to the nation and to all the people what was in my heart that night—With God's help and yours I would do the best I could.

I was proud that the first citizen who called upon me to offer his strength and his support was General Dwight David Eisenhower. He spent more than two hours in my office with a lead pencil and a yellow tablet, writing his suggestions.

And then from Independence came that happy warrior, President Harry Truman.

I am very grateful and very humble that in this critical hour, I had the trust of men like Bob Taft, Bill Knowland, and Everett Dirksen.

Everett Dirksen supported the test ban treaty in a critical hour in the Senate when without his support it may not have become law, when the present Republican candidate was fighting it. Together, Everett Dirksen and John F. Kennedy passed that treaty that 105 nations ratified that makes the air that you breathe safer and the milk that you drink cleaner.

I want every businessman who believes in profits and prudence, every labor man who wants adequate wages and reasonable working conditions, to get out and do some heavy thinking now.

Finally, it was just 2 years ago that I sat around the Cabinet table in the Cuban missile crisis. In that room we knew no parties. We knew we were only Americans. And Mr. Khrushchev and Mr. Kennedy stood there eyeball to eyeball, each with a knife in the other one's ribs, and neither quivering or quaking. There was no palsy in their hands.

There were a lot of hotheads all around the place. But as those generals came in with the stars on their shoulders, and the admirals walked down the corridors with the gold on their braid, I am proud to tell you that the coolest customer, the wisest man in that room, was the man that you, in your wisdom, the masses of the people, had selected to be your Commander in Chief, John Fitzgerald Kennedy.

I was a Congressman for 12 years. I was a Senator for 12 years. I was leader of my party for 8 years. I was Vice President for over 3 years, as President Kennedy's assistant and his helper. But you will go and vote not for Lyndon Johnson and not for the Democratic Party. You will go vote for yourself and your family.

I know when I am sitting down there on the banks of the river in my little house near where I was born on the Pedernales River in Texas, I know that they will tell me that you voted for what you knew in your heart was right.

Johnson was a crude, coarse, tall, lanky Texan and a political evangelist who wanted the greatest landslide in history as he carried his message into America's heartland. As he spoke, a number of Goldwater signs were ripped apart.

It was widely reported that he was always late to everything, and he was late in starting this talk as well. One reason he was always late was that he loved the telephone. He was always calling people up himself, and wanting them to be instantly available to him (even if they were on the pot). He'd say, so the press reported, "I don't care where he is. I'm the president and I want to talk to him right now." And, of course, it was hard for anyone to resist him or his requests for their help which might come at any hour of the day or night.

He sidestepped controversial issues and relied instead on safer "peace and prosperity" themes. He ignored his own pleas to guard against over-confidence and shouted to the crowd to give "Lyndon Johnson and Hubert Humphrey the greatest victory in history."

However, later he addressed union delegates at the Peoria Armory and admitted to uneasiness about political polls, which favored him. He recalled how polls once had favored Thomas Dewey, who was later upset by Truman. When finally elected, he did have a landslide and Goldwater was, of course, overwhelmed.

That day, when I returned to the *Star-Courier* office in Kewanee, Illinois, I wrote two drafts, the first portraying him as a biblical prophet pleading with the multitude to save the world from destruction by voting for him. This was almost true, but after a good laugh, I toned it down a few decibels. He didn't make a brilliant talk, but a gutsy one.

Johnson declined to run for another term because of problems over the Vietnam War and left office embittered. I feel that the thousands of crosses in the jungles of Southeast Asia and the names on the Vietnam Memorial in Washington, D.C., attest to being part of Johnson's legacy.

I took one other photograph of Johnson as he used some of his Texas humor to amuse the audience and assembled politicians.

Some people may think I am a little tough on Johnson, but let me remind you that Harry Truman once said Lyndon Johnson did "more to weaken the presidency than any man in this century" through his conduct of the Vietnam War and his decision not to seek re-election. Thomas Fleming in *American Heritage* magazine said that Truman gave this opinion of Johnson in a 1970 interview when he was 86 years old. Truman felt Johnson should have run again and made the election a referendum on the Vietnam War as Lincoln did during the Civil War.

Fleming wrote that any man who weakened the presidency was bad. If Johnson had run for re-election in 1968, the voters could decide whether they wanted war or peace in Vietnam. But instead, Johnson allowed anti-war protestors to claim that they drove him to resign. Truman added that Johnson had "no guts!"

Did he have guts? Early on, imitating his mother's flowery speech and fancy dress left him feeling sissified and cowardly. He avoided fights even though he was bigger than most boys. This gave him some doubts about his manliness, which would prove to be the secret of his unwillingness to pull forces out of Viet Nam.

He proclaimed at the onset of World War II, "I shall never vote for war and then hide behind a House seat where bullets cannot reach me," but he did. To help his political career, he requested to visit shipyards and was sent on one military combat flight where his plane was shot at. As time went by, Johnson exaggerated his military duty and a case of flu became Dengue Fever. His 25-pound weight loss became 40 pounds. The 20,000 miles he had flown became 60,000. The one mission he flew became missions. The 13 minutes of actual combat became three months. He gave himself the nickname "Raider Johnson" and wore a Silver Star on his regular attire, often pulling his lapel to show it during speeches.

His quest for approval of the masses was bigger than life because he wanted to be remembered in history as the greatest Congressman, the greatest Senator, and the greatest President. After Kennedy's assassination, he worried that he might be a target and the famous telephone interview with FBI director J. Edgar Hoover revealed his fears only days after taking office as the President.

After his heart attack in 1955, he didn't want to sleep alone for fear he'd die alone, so if Ladybird was away, he would have an aide sleep with him. The day he died, nobody was around and he took a nap alone from which he never awoke.

Lyndon B. Johnson (August 27, 1908-January 22, 1973) was our 36th president, serving with Vice President Hubert Humphrey.

Chapter Five

Richard Milhous Nixon

Nixon—Astuteness in foreign affairs.

Richard Nixon hurt himself more than he hurt the country in Watergate. Senator George McGovern, soundly beaten by Nixon in 1972, said the tragedy of Watergate was that Nixon probably was the most qualified candidate ever elected in modern history.

Although I have had personal interviews with the last eleven U.S. presidents and also have photographed each, most people still appear to have an undying interest in Richard M. Nixon, one of the most controversial presidents in years.

I did get a fair amount of notoriety during the Watergate years when an editorial I wrote for the Ottumwa, Iowa, Courier as a "Plea for Sanity" was reprinted in 573 newspapers across the country. Here I was with an Irish, Catholic, Democratic family background and I was one of the few who supported Nixon.

It got so much attention that our newspaper printed three issues of it because they kept selling out. The Iowa Public Radio system called the next morning to find out what was happening as they received many calls about the editorial. Hon. Robert H. Michel, speaker of the house in the Illinois House of Representatives, had it printed in the Congressional Record on November 8, 1973. He prefaced it with these words:

> I want to bring to the attention of my colleagues the editorial opinion of an old friend of mine, now publisher of the *Courier* in

Ottumwa, Iowa. In a time like this when all we seem to be getting from much of the media is something akin to hysteria, it is refreshing to see that Jerry Moriarity is still displaying that good, old-fashioned brand of horse sense that we all need to help us put things in perspective and use reason and good judgment in our evaluation of what is happening nationally. I insert his editorial, "A Plea for Sanity" at this point in the Record.

And shortly, "All Things Considered" of National Public Radio in Washington, D.C., called for an interview, which resulted in five prime time interviews by Susan Stamberg, a talented interviewer who asked me great questions. In fact, she kept calling me for interviews on a weekly basis, even when I was spending the summer at our lake home on Little Pine Lake near Perham, Minnesota. I had one call at a Rotary meeting when I had a tape recorder with me, so I played it for the membership who liked it because I mentioned that the lake was noted for its great Walleye fishing.

Later, an official of the Associated Press in New York called to say my Nixon story was the most widely reprinted editorial on Watergate. And it paid one quick dividend as Nixon invited me to the White House for what turned out to be a Prayer Breakfast session with many national leaders.

As guests paraded in a line to meet the president, they were urged just to shake hands and move on. It didn't work that way for me as Nixon thanked me for the editorial support and then wanted to talk about Ottumwa, Iowa, where he was a Naval officer before going overseas.

Later, I learned that he was an astute poker player and helped finance his first political campaign for Congress with his winnings. He had learned poker and cussing first in Prescott, Arizona, and later in the Navy. He spent teenage summers in Prescott because his mother nursed his oldest brother, who suffered and finally died of tuberculosis, in a sanitarium (with good dry clean air) two blocks from the town square. Nixon spent his vacation time as a janitor at a country club and barker at a carnival. He visited the famous Palace Bar, a saloon on the square, where he picked up poker and cuss words, which came to public attention in some White House tapes.

Nixon was in an expansive mood as we chatted and I remember him telling me "Good friends are the best, aren't they?" With impeachment looming, he probably wished he had more friends.

Our conversation went on at length and I could hear someone in the back ask, "What's taking so long?" And the reply was, "He found someone he wanted to talk to." It made for a rather heady day for an Iowa newsman.

So much for the accolades.

I had five or six meetings with Nixon and some of them were very memorable. I will go into more detail later, but I got into his good graces when I wrote the editorial defending him.

During World War II when Nixon was an officer at the Naval Aviation base in Ottumwa, his wife, Patricia, worked at the main Ottumwa bank. She accompanied him when I met him in Minneapolis, Minnesota, where he addressed a national secretary's convention. As vice president then, he mostly defended President Eisenhower sending troops to Lebanon. Among other cities where I met Nixon was Kewanee, Illinois, where he spoke at a Barry Goldwater rally when Goldwater was a presidential candidate opposing Lyndon Johnson.

On October 30, 1964, a crowd of 3,000 assembled to hear Nixon. A slow motorcade from Kewanee to the Moline-Rock Island airport accounted for a late start. This was the last stop in a six-city Illinois tour by the former vice president. All along the route, Nixon called for a victory for presidential candidate Sen. Barry M. Goldwater and the Illinois Republican ticket. He praised Goldwater as a man of character and called for new direction in foreign policy. Nixon warned that communism still is on the upswing despite peace messages of new Soviet leaders. He said the messages to President Lyndon B. Johnson "are not worth the paper they're written on."

He said, "On Nov. 3 I'll be sitting back listening to the returns and paying particular attention to the 36 states I campaigned in. But the state I really want to see come through -- and you know why -- is Illinois."

"I do not question Mr. Humphrey's loyalty to his country or his devotion to peace," Nixon said. "He just happens to be a very sincere, very dedicated radical." He also compared the "character" of Goldwater and Johnson, and said that Goldwater would "provide moral as well as legal leadership for the nation."

It was Nixon's fourth appearance in Rockford since 1952. He last was here during the 1960 presidential campaign when he spoke at a rally in the National Guard Armory.

Nixon often was depicted as an evil genius, but I feel when he passes the scrubbing board of history, more of his good traits will be revealed. You have to go back to 1969 to learn something very favorable about Nixon. That was the year that the government took in more money than it spent. Despite the cost of the Vietnam War, the government's budget was only $184 billion. What did Nixon do? He used the $187 billion collected from taxpayers to fund important federal programs and keep the budget down. This was the next to last time the U.S. had a balanced budget.

Being a press man, I always enjoyed what William Safire said about Nixon. Safire was the public relations man for the company that built the typical American kitchen at the U.S. Exhibition in Moscow. He brilliantly got Nikita Khrushchev and Richard Nixon into his client's kitchen. Nixon left the kitchen after his famous debate with Khrushchev, telling Safire that they had put his kitchen on the map and he ought to visit him to talk. Then Safire became one of three speechwriters for Nixon.

Nixon's favorite jokes were about farmers and no wonder since he had to buy produce for his father's grocery store in California from local farmers and knew animals as well as profanity. The hottest part of the encounter between Nixon and Khrushchev involved the following profane statements. The Russian premier became enraged and ridiculed Nixon for the Captive Nations Resolution that had been passed shortly before the vice president left for Europe.

Khrushchev told Nixon that the Soviet Union would never issue such a statement and that he was "bewildered" by such congressional actions, which would only cause more problems between the U.S. and the U.S.S.R. Nixon tried to change the subject but Khrushchev persevered and told him the resolution "stinks like fresh horse shit, and nothing smells worse than that."

Nixon remembered that Khrushchev began life as a pig breeder and crudely said, "I am afraid the Chairman is mistaken. There is something that smells worse than horse shit and that is pig shit." Khrushchev was angered, tried to smile, and finally agreed to change the subject. Continuing the debate, Khrushchev criticized Nixon for supporting McCarthy earlier in his career and again criticized Nixon for the Captive Nations Resolution. But the debate then took a quieter tone about the nature of each country's technological innovations.

The year of 1972 was another great one for Nixon. That was when Nixon entered into secret negotiations with Chairman Mao Tse-Tung of China and some observers contend his tour changed the world.

This was the first time since 1949 when the leaders of China and the U.S. had met. It turned out to be important that the United States had never occupied China and Mao told an aide that he favored meeting America's right wingers because they mean what they say.

Even though Nixon was humiliated because of Watergate, he once delivered a brilliant speech on TV (which I saw), to a huge crowd, many of whom had been his "enemies" and they gave him a standing ovation. I can't remember the date but it was unreal—and too late!

By the way, Nixon did send me autographed copies of two of his books and he in the following letter invited me to visit him. I still regret my failure to do that. What a lost opportunity.

RICHARD NIXON

LA CASA PACIFICA
SAN CLEMENTE, CALIFORNIA

March 6, 1979

Dear Mr. Moriarty,
Your letter of February 22 brought back
many pleasant memories. I am presently
writing a book on foreign policy which will
be published this fall. Should you be
travelling to this area in October or
November I would enjoy a visit. I would
suggest that you check with my assistant,
Colonel Jack Brennan, to work out a
mutually convenient time.

It occurred to me that you might like a
copy of my Memoirs for your personal
library and I am sending one under separate
cover appropriately inscribed.

With warm regards,

Sincerely,

Richard Nixon

Mr. Jerry Moriarity
Ottumwa Courier
Ottumwa, Iowa 52501

**Nixon's invitation of March 6, 1979, to visit
him at San Clemente, California.**

**I didn't take Nixon's offer to visit San Clemente,
but I visited his birthplace in Yorba Linda.**

I talked with Richard Nixon when he was in town to support Barry Goldwater for president in his run against Lyndon Johnson.

Richard and Pat Nixon

Richard Nixon had the distinction of being the first president to resign. His name and career will forever be linked to what was at first called a third-rate burglary at Watergate. But that third-rate burglary has a longer shelf-life than uranium. President Ford's memorials when he died in 2006 resurrected every unsavory tidbit about Nixon that the press could find.

I decided one time to visit the National Public Radio offices to prove I wasn't a Neanderthal because of my stand on Nixon. The crew provided a receptionist to take me around the office. It was interesting, of course, until I saw the main studio microphone. Beside the mike was a printed card in large type which said, "Impeach Nixon." So when Susan Stamberg called me on the day that Nixon resigned, she asked for my reaction. I started out all right until that "impeach" sign came booming back into my memory. I really goofed and lost all coherence. So I called back to say I wanted to revise my comments, but I was just as bad that second time when I questioned the impartiality of my hosts. All I needed to say was, "It was Nixon's decision, not mine." But I still think Susan Stamberg was great.

Nixon himself was a unique and unlikely character ever to be elected president. He had detractors when he pursued persons with Communistic leanings. He got national attention in 1948 as a member of the House Un-American Activities Committee. Yet few people, even now, recognize that Nixon had a very high intelligence and was perhaps the smartest president at least in modern times except for Bill Clinton. Nixon's IQ was once measured at 143 which qualifies him for Mensa and places him in the top one percent of the population in intelligence. In comparison, John Kennedy had an IQ of 118, one point above his assassin, Lee Harvey Oswald (117), and both were simply high average.

In my meetings with Nixon I noticed that he seemed more comfortable meeting and chatting with just a few people than a crowd. He did have the ability to turn on the charm. Once in the White House for that prayer breakfast, he spotted a little negro child and bent over to chat. She beamed as did her mother when Nixon confided to the girl that she could have seconds on the food and goodies being served.

Not everyone agreed with my editorial defending Nixon. Some readers in other states sent it back with obscene comments. However, one stated "Moriarity for President," obviously a minority view but I appreciated it. Many of my friends couldn't understand how I could defend Nixon. My reply was that I didn't sell my soul; only that I rented it.

A Plea for Sanity:

Has our perspective been lost?

By Jerry Moriarity

Publisher, the *Ottumwa Courier*

October 24, 1973

Will not one sane voice be raised in these United States with a plea for reasonableness in judging President Richard Nixon?

Will not just one politician abandon the vitriolic, hysteria-creating rhetoric long enough to ask what is being done to our country? And why?

Will not just one editor, embraced by his own obsessions over a shield law, honestly admit that others, even Presidents, have rights to privacy also? Even on tape.

As an interested observer on the presidential scene since the days of Harry S Truman (although earlier I had heard and seen both Franklin D. Roosevelt and Al Smith—but not at the same time) it is distressing to see how this once vigorous nation is being torn asunder in the wake of the sordid Watergate debacle.

Nixon now is being condemned as a Hitler-figure, as an immoral politician, incapable of leading this nation. Impeachment looms on the horizon.

Somehow the perspective has been lost completely.

Just how great are his crimes? How many lives have been lost? How many tax dollars have been misappropriated? How many elected officials have been contaminated?

And let's compare Nixon with several of his predecessors, too, while we're at it.

I was in Washington, D.C., in the new State Department building a number of years ago on the exact day President John F. Kennedy confessed to us that American pilots were flying missions for the first time in South Vietnam.

Before that, under President Eisenhower, we had only an advisory role. Now we were projected—by presidential decree—into that of actual combatants. The pilots who died on those first sweeps started a parade of dead that later seemed interminable. And the war itself was almost interminable, made so because of the no-win policies inflicted on our fighting men.

And don't forget we had the ill-conceived and ill-fated Bay of Pigs invasion of Cuba, engineered by Kennedy, who let the Cuban patriots die on the beaches because no American fire or air power had been supplied as promised. Not even the New York Times protested! And there were no cries for impeachment.

Does the arrest of the four Cubans in the Watergate burglary match this tragedy as some commentators would have us believe?

I heard President Lyndon Johnson in Peoria, condemning Barry Goldwater as a warmonger, while proclaiming himself as a disciple of peace. Many of us still remember the distasteful TV commercials of the little girl with a daisy being blown up in an atomic holocaust, all because of Goldwater, according to the Johnson scriptwriters. Johnson once said: "I'm President of the United States and I can do any goddam thing I want to." And he did. So it wasn't surprising that in a few months after his election, the Messiah of peace out-Goldwatered Goldwater, hobbling us in a war unlike any other in our history.

I felt at the time that Johnson was a dangerous hypocrite and the thousands of crosses in the jungles of Southeast Asia now attest to that truth. And surprisingly—or is it surprisingly?—the fawning liberal press praised Johnson as a hero upon his death. Impeachment never crossed their minds.

Yet these same critics are yelping at Nixon's heels, even though it was Nixon who brought that ugly war to a conclusion.

For the first time in a generation America is at peace. For the first time in more than a score of years, no American serviceman is dying in combat.

And it was Nixon who broke down the barriers separating the U.S. from both Red China and the Soviet Union, no small accomplishment under any standards.

To understand Watergate, it is wise to reflect on the America Nixon inherited as President. Cities were burning. Weathermen revolutionaries were blowing up buildings, occasionally themselves. Civil disobedience was the pattern. President Johnson could not even attend the Democratic convention in Chicago, so ugly was the mood. Candidate Eugene McCarthy couldn't get from his hotel to the convention hall because of demonstrators on the streets. Hippies rioted in the parks, foul words written on their foreheads; some with their pants' fronts opened, exposing themselves. Others contented themselves with throwing human waste at the harassed Chicago police. I was happy to get away from that scene.

And can you honestly say conditions in the U.S. are worse now under Nixon? You've got to be lying in your teeth!

Honk for impeachment, if you will. The sounds can be heard again over the still land; a few years ago they would have been drowned in the cacophony of discontent.

* * *

I've got one more comment to make about Nixon. Gabriel Byrne, the Irish actor who plays a psychiatrist on the current HBO hit "In Treatment," told about meeting Richard Nixon at a ball game when Nixon was no longer the president. Nixon loved to attend ball games, I've heard. Byrne recognized him and tried to find something to hand him to autograph. He approached the ex-president with a liner from the cigarette package. Nixon was still protected by Secret Service agents. They waved him off saying something like you can't get an autograph on a cigarette package. But Nixon heard the comment and said he would sign the cigarette paper and Byrne is the proud owner of that autograph.

Richard M. Nixon (January 9, 1913-August 9, 1974) was our 37th president, serving from 1969-74 with Vice President Spiro Agnew first and then Gerald Ford.

Chapter Six

Gerald Rudolph Ford

Ford: Decency

Gerald Ford was probably the most decent individual who could serve in the trying days following the agony of Watergate. Everyone who ever described meeting him had the same kind of description. He was modest, never intended to be president, believed strongly in majority opinion, and cared naught about his own reputation or future legacy as evidenced by his pardon of Nixon. Even Anwar Sadat, third president of Egypt before he was assassinated, was impressed by Gerald Ford's genuine kindness and interest in peace.

When Ford assumed office after the resignation by Richard Nixon, he became the first vice president and president who had not been elected to either office.

He was virtually in a no-win situation after pardoning Nixon, which he preferred doing rather than have the Watergate problem fester throughout his term. To his credit Ford continued to do the best he could.

Somehow I was able to cover Ford at four different locations. I covered a speech by him in Omaha, Nebraska, when he was promoting his WIN program (Whip Inflation Now). A friend, Al Pinder of Grinnell, Iowa, got us there early to get better seats. As usual I carried a camera. But when I got up to check on activity in another room, I almost wasn't able to get back to my place.

A security guard insisted I take the camera apart. I told him I already had been inside and could not open the camera without exposing the film. After a long hassle he finally let me back in with the camera intact.

A couple of Jerrys, President Gerald R. Ford, chatting with me in Minneapolis in October, 1974.

Ford also came to Mason City, Iowa, when I was publisher of the *Globe-Gazette*. Later, he had breakfast with executives of Lee Enterprise in Minneapolis. A special event occurred when Hubert Humphrey, longtime Minneapolis mayor and vice president under Johnson, showed up to greet Ford. Humphrey was fighting the burden of cancer and was not his usual vibrant and vivacious self. It was sad seeing him because when I was active in the Jaycees we often had him as convention speaker. He was a dynamo and we considered him as Wisconsin's third senator.

I'll take a moment to add some things I remember about Humphrey. When he was the subject of a press roast in Minneapolis in 1976, he said, "As for me, I can only tell you I am not a candidate for president. I've made 31 appearances in California only because I like Disneyland." He also added, "I must be a candidate; otherwise why are they saying all these scurrilous things about me." Never one to abbreviate comments, his Muriel said about his marriage proposal, "I accepted four times before he finished."

President Ford invited delegates from the 15th annual government affairs conference, sponsored by the National Newspaper Association, to the White House March 19, 1976. During the televised session, Ford invited questions from the audience after his opening remarks. During his brief talk, Ford warned about Congress' failure to correct defects in campaign reform laws, and he also joyously announced that the cost of living figure for February represented the lowest increase in four years.

I was the publisher of the *Ottumwa Courier* then and asked him one question which brought laughter and praise for newspapers. I hoped to get the President's reaction to press coverage and also his opinion about newspapers specifically. My question and his response were given in the official transcript released by the White House:

QUESTION: Mr. President, as long as most of us in this room are in the newspaper business, and your daughter Susan served on a newspaper in Kansas, how has your opinion of the newspaper business changed?

THE PRESIDENT: I love the newspapers (Laughter) and I love the people that do the reporting, too. (Laughter) We get along very well, and I am an avid reader of newspapers, to tell you the truth. I think they do a fine job, and I also think the people who cover the White House do a fine job. We don't always agree. I like some headlines better than the others, but they have a responsibility and I have one, and I think we understand each one and our respective responsibilities.

By the way, our seats were virtually perfect. The six Moriaritys occupied an entire front row. After the conference, the guests had access to the first floor and lower level of the mansion, and refreshments were served in the State dining room. For a time the President wandered about, chatting and giving autographs.

Although cameras were discouraged, the pocket Instamatics popped out from everything. Our daughter, Kathleen, a research analyst in the Department of Justice, almost cracked up when she heard her 15-year-old brother, Tim, cheerfully ordering the President to "smile" as he tried for a happy pose. "Unbelievable," was all she could say.

Both Tim and Joe, 10, also got the President's autographs on their registration tags. Joe asked to borrow my inexpensive ballpoint pen for the occasion, but the President kept using it to sign others. Dutifully I trotted along behind until I finally said (with a chuckle, you understand), "I'm going to stay with you until I get my pen back. It's worth more now than it was before."

After he signed the next autograph, he turned around with a broad grin and said, "Here, I'll use my own." So the pen with the symbol and words of "Rock Island Lines" came back into my possession.

Later as we nibbled on the delicious pastries, Joe solemnly declared, "Dad, I got President Ford's autograph, but I forgot to shake his hand." Offering a challenge, I merely replied, "Well, you should know what to do about that."

In seconds, Joe had burrowed through the crowd and ended looking up at the President. Ford leaned over, read Joe's name tag, and asked, "You're from Ottumwa, aren't you?"

After saying, "Yes," Joe confessed, "I got your autograph before, but forgot to shake your hand."

They shook and a mighty excited lad came running back with a memory that will long endure.

One of the articles I wrote after returning from that conference was the following:

Fishy Conference

It wouldn't be entirely facetious to say there was something fishy about the opening day's program at the 15ᵗʰ Annual Government Affairs Conference, sponsored in Washington, D.C., by the National Newspaper Association.

We had Pike for breakfast and Muskie for lunch—and it wasn't even Friday.

Pike, of course, is U.S. Rep. Otis Pike, democrat from New York and critic of the Central Intelligence Agency. The other was Sen. Edmund S. Muskie (D-Maine).

It is Pike who will have our attention in today's article and later in the series we will balance it with comments from George Bush, newly appointed director of the controversial CIA.

Pike has been the vortex of a swirling argument because of his role as chairman of the House Select Committee on Intelligence. Although he and his committee, mostly along party lines, favored publication of their investigative report on the CIA, their colleagues in Congress voted against them in national interests. Pike's reaction was clearly stated. He was "personally outraged."

Pike insists that the report should have been made public (actually it was, through a leak to the *Village Voice* newspaper by Daniel Schorr) because of the cost of intelligence work, the risks involved, and results of such operations.

He argues rather convincingly that the CIA failed on six major crises: The Soviet invasion of Czechoslovakia, the Tet offensive in South Vietnam, the Arab-Israeli Yom Kippur War, Cyprus' coup, Portugal's coup, and India's explosion of a nuclear device. (Director Bush disputed this charge at his later conference.)

The greatest peril facing the nation is the feeling, according to Pike, that "many people believe the government does not tell the truth."

In arguing against the practice of stamping too many documents "secret", Pike states, "No agreement which is not supported by the American people is valid...Printing the truth will always be better than suppressing it."

After declaring the American people should have the right to know, he continued, "It is always my judgment that the public has a right to know almost everything."

The "almost" has more than two syllables when it comes to interpretation.

Under questioning, Pike admitted names of intelligence agents should be kept secret. Sources and methods also should be kept under wraps and communications between heads of governments must be protected.

Pike believes that not all covert operations of the CIA should be barred, but he said no assassination attempts should be permitted, members of the press and clergy should not be utilized to convey or receive information, and there should be no paramilitary operations in peacetime.

Time after time, the questioning came around to how Pike would classify secrets and who would decide.

Most of the replies were vague or obscure.

Eventually I joined the questioners and asked, "My question is who should be the ultimate authority, the one person, to decide upon the validity of such secrets?"

Pike replied it should be a joint operation of the executive and legislative branches. "I would always allow the executive branch (on behalf of the President) to make arguments, but I would never let it exercise veto power." How Congress would handle intelligence secrets never was clearly explained.

Pike did state, however, "there has to be a better system than leaks to inform the American public."

Most of our family was invited to meet President Ford in the White House one year. Somehow I had a photo of the Watergate complex in my pocket, but I had no idea why I had it.

Then I noticed one of the guests asked Ford for his autograph and he immediately glanced around to see the closest exit. Each time he moved I also moved. Finally he came within a few steps of me so I pulled out the Watergate photo and asked him to sign it.

If I had been him, I probably would have rewarded this impertinence with a punch to the jaw, but he graciously signed it.

Several people around me couldn't believe I did this, but after all, his whole destiny was entwined around Watergate.

That was the same visit that I attended a ceremonial given for the Prime Minister of Ireland by President Ford on St. Patrick's Day, March 17, 1976. Liam Cosgrove's visit was considered a timely tribute to the American Bicentennial and he stressed a common devotion to freedom. His appearance at an outdoor program was brightened by the colorful pageantry of military honor guards, including a Revolutionary War-style drum and fife united.

After the arrival of the prime minister and his wife by helicopter at the Ellipse (the White House park), he was brought by limousine to the south lawn near the executive mansion. Both Ford and Cosgrove conducted inspections of the military services.

Most of the Moriarity clan (there were six of us there that day) were in the area adjacent to the representatives of the Irish embassy. Irish and American flags were awarded before the playing of *Ruffles and Flourishes*, a musical salute, *Hail to the Chief*, and then the national anthems of both countries. The music gave a warming tingle to the otherwise chilly weather.

In his public remarks, Cosgrove noted, "It is particularly appropriate that our visit should commence on St. Patrick's Day, which has a special significance for Ireland and, indeed, also for the United States."

Because of this, Ford probably could be excused from indulging in what could be called benign ethnic politics. He told Cosgrove, "I welcome you not only as prime minister of Ireland, but as a kinsman, very distant in genealogy, but very close in affinity. My mother proudly told me one time I am partially Irish in heritage and I can assure you, I am fully Irish in spirit."

When we got back in the White House later, several staff members we met were still talking about the party that night. Actor Pat O'Brien and Sen. Ted Kennedy were among the more authentic Irishers at the dinner. The senator brought his daughter, Kara, 16, in place of his wife who was ill with the flu. Also attending were Dick Cheney, a Ford staff member, and Donald Rumsfeld, Ford's chief of staff. But most importantly, the lovely Zsa Zsa Gabor added glamour to Ford's personal table. (The Democrats should give Ford credit for being smarter than they say he is. After all, Kissinger, Ford's Secretary of State, used to get all the goodies.) For those interested in trivia, the society writers of Washington noted that Zsa Zsa "tippytoed with Ford and she sighed, 'Anyone who dances with President Ford will vote for him; he is such a marvelous dancer'."

In actuality, Ford was one of our most athletic presidents. He was a Michigan star in football, but former president Johnson always accused him of playing too long without a helmet. Unfortunately, comedians such as Chevy Chase made him out as a klutz.

On that same trip in March, 1976, we worked in a visit to the Indonesian Embassy where we sampled fried bananas. Indonesia was in the news because, with the support of Secretary of State Kissinger and President Ford, they had invaded East Timor three months earlier. That invasion led to the death of nearly one-third of the population of East Timor. President Ford, when asked by reporters in the 1990s whether he had supported the invasion said, "I'm sorry, I just don't remember," which sounds genuine to me. I believe he was basically a very good man who would not have wanted to be responsible for the massacre which occurred.

When Gerald Ford died in 2006, the newspapers printed what he had to say about other presidents. The *Grand Rapids Press* reported his comments over a 25-year period and I was interested to find that his evaluations were very close to my own. On January 13, 2007, they printed the column taken from the Associated Press entitled "The Late Gerald Ford Pulled No Punches When Rating Presidents."

He said of Harry Truman, "Look at what he faced. There was the challenge of Korea in 1951. He had no hesitancy using atomic weapons (on) Hiroshima and Nagasaki. He came up with the Marshall Plan, which saved Europe after World War II… He deserves high marks."

He said about Dwight Eisenhower, "The best president of my lifetime… The Soviets under Stalin were an aggressive, formidable military operation. NATO, under Ike, stopped them… Overall, the economy under him was in pretty good shape for eight years."

He commented about John Kennedy, "He had a tremendous following, but I think the substance of his presidency was not as good as it was professed to be… Kennedy would never have gotten the civil rights legislation through."

He critiqued Lyndon Johnson saying, "Lyndon, despite his personal eccentricities, did a lot of good things… At times, while he was president and I was (House) minority leader, he was unfair and too tough on me…. He was caught up in the worst aspects of the Vietnam syndrome. He inherited a policy that started with Kennedy, and he didn't want to break it off. And it kept getting worse."

He had interesting insight into Richard Nixon saying, "On foreign policy, he was the best of (the 20th) century. He was very intelligent and very strong… Nixon was a bad president when it came to picking some of his top people—Haldeman, Ehrlichman, Colson… Nixon made a few mistakes. He was so stubborn that he would never concede or admit that he had made them. And they steamrolled."

He commented briefly on Jimmy Carter saying, "I feel very strongly that Jimmy Carter was a disaster, particularly domestically and economically. I have said more than once that he was certainly the poorest president in my lifetime."

He had limited compliments for Ronald Reagan saying, "A great spokesman for attractive political objectives. The American people liked to hear him talk about a balanced budget. They liked to hear him talk about how good America was and how bad communism was but, when it came to implementation, his record never matched his words."

He had interesting comments about George H. W. Bush saying, "A good president… He handled the Saddam Hussein conflict very skillfully… He didn't realize, or his people didn't realize, that the economy was in trouble… By the time the Bush administration woke up, the Democrats had the issue and Bush never got it back."

He had great foresight into Bill Clinton saying, "Probably as skillful an articulator of politics since Franklin D. Roosevelt. I have grave reservations about his convictions but, when you come to being a salesman, he's about as good as it gets… I think he will come out as an average president, overall… He never had the substance, the will power to face up to a crisis."

While I am discussing his ratings, I'll just add a little more. Ranking of U.S. presidents is a fascinating game that lots of historians enjoy playing. One would almost always think that George Washington would remain number one in the ranking. But that is not always true. But is interesting to know how the eleven presidents I interviewed would rank. I obtained two different lists of rankings—one was from *C-Span*, and the other was a combination of the Federalist Society and the *Wall Street Journal* rankings.

In 1999, *C-Span* ranked Harry Truman number five just behind Abraham Lincoln, Franklin Roosevelt, George Washington and Theodore Roosevelt. Not bad for Truman who once had a lower presidential rating than the current president, George W. Bush, so there may be hope for "W" if the Iraq war ever comes to an end. *C-Span* ranked the other presidents I interviewed as follows: Kennedy—8, Eisenhower—9, Johnson—10, Reagan—11, George H. Bush—20, Clinton—21, Carter—22, Ford—23, Nixon—25.

In 2000, James Lindgren asked academic scholars of the Federalist Society to rank the presidents and their results were categorized into Great, Near Great, Above Average, Average, Below Average, and Failure. In the Near Greats were Reagan—6, Truman—7, Eisenhower—8. In the Above Average was John Kennedy—15. In the Average were Lyndon Johnson—18, and George W. Bush—19 (remember this was done in 2000), George H. W. Bush—21, and Clinton—22. In the Below Average were Gerald Ford—28, Richard Nixon—32, and Jimmy Carter—34.

Our Ex-PRESS Club in Sun City West had Bob Cheney, a well-known historian in Arizona, speak to the group, whose name has now been changed to the Media Club of the West Valley. Cheney is also the author of *Hood's Texas Brigade* and *Brushes with Greatness*. Some of his thoughts about ranking are these:

> I would rank Truman as the 5th most important president, and in a tie for the 10th most important president are Lyndon Johnson, Richard Nixon, and Ronald Reagan. In my ten worst presidents, I believe that Carter is 8th, Nixon is 9th, and Lyndon Johnson is 10th. Yes, sometimes I think an "important" president can also be a "bad" president. Once George W. Bush completes his terms, he will immediately jump to the top of my worst list replacing Ulysses S. Grant who leads my list as the worst president ever. I would rank the eleven presidents you interviewed from best to worst in this order: Harry Truman, Lyndon Johnson, Richard Nixon, Ronald Reagan, Dwight Eisenhower, Bill Clinton, John Kennedy, George H. W. Bush, Gerald Ford, Jimmy Carter, and George W. Bush. Lyndon, a crude jerk, was second because of his Great Society program, Medicare, and all the things he made happen.

Ford was an amiable individual and certainly a most decent gentleman. Gerald R. Ford (July 14, 1913-December 26, 2006) was our 38th president, serving from 1974-77 with Vice President Nelson Rockefeller.

Chapter Seven

Jimmy Carter

Carter: Ethical

Jimmy Carter was an intelligent but insecure person, a victim of the very platform on which he ran, an anti-Washington stand. This put him at odds with the power structure, which never accepted his Georgia "Mafia." He created a high moral image nonetheless.

One thing that can be said about Carter without fear of contradiction is that he has become a better past president than president.

After Carter was elected, Lee Enterprise officials poked fun at me. The president of Lee at that time was Lloyd Schermer, a good associate who cooperated with me in many ventures in Illinois including a campaign to curtail invasions by the strip-miners. We never applied, but Lloyd always felt we would have won a Pulitzer if we had.

Well, at this Florida convention, Lloyd called me to the front of the convention hall and after a few choice, but hilarious, remarks made a presentation to me, because he said, "Jerry will never again be invited back to the White House since Carter was elected."

He then made a presentation of a book entitled "How I Influenced the Election of Jimmy Carter by Jerry Moriarity." It was a beautifully printed publication with a gold title inscription on a rich red cover.

The joke, of course, was that the book had all empty pages.

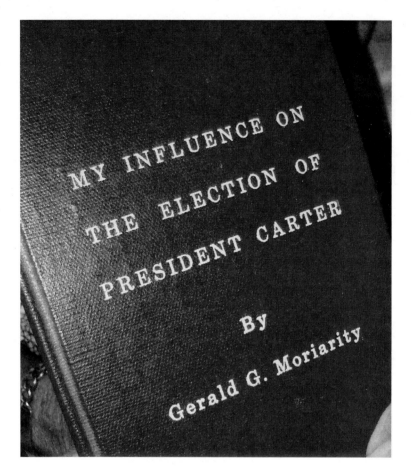

The no text book I was awarded in 1977.

But, surprise, I was invited to the White House by Jimmy Carter and took the book along with me. Before going to the White House, our first sessions were in the Old Executive Building next door.

We had a steady parade of cabinet members so I took the opportunity of having them sign their autographs. And I also did the same with some of the press representatives.

Pat Barrio, press secretary, saw what I was doing and she asked about it and even got a chuckle as she said that I could not take the book into the White House, but if I wanted to, she would try to have Carter autograph it.

I offered to give her money for postage, which she refused, and I thought, "Yes, there goes more federal money down the tube."

We had another tour of the White House and learned our meeting with Carter would be in the cabinet room.

You can guess what happened next as I abandoned our group, located the cabinet room and asked a guide at the door where the president usually sits. He told me the president sits in a chair that is about two inches higher than all the rest.

When the group trotted into the cabinet room, I plopped down next to the president's "throne." Then I described to him how I started a campaign to have Ottumwa, Iowa, named an All-America City.

He said (Friday, November 11, 1977) that he encouraged the Ottumwas of the nation, which have worked to better themselves and striven to attain All-America honors.

Best wishes to Jerry Moriarity

Jimmy Carter

**President Jimmy and Rosalynn Carter in the
White House with me November 11, 1977.**

In the next day's Walter Cronkite news program, a close-up of
Carter and me was shown on national television but I did not see
it as I was flying to Denver to address the All-America city judges.
My plea, accompanied by a visual slide show, earned honors for Ottumwa. My approach as always was to "put the word UNITY back
into CommUNITY."

Carter also gave us, there in the Cabinet Room, a summary of
his address to the Nation on Energy made three days earlier. He
described the tremendous outpouring of American dollars to buy
oil from foreign countries. He said, "If this trend continues, the ex-

cessive reliance on foreign oil could make the very security of our Nation increasingly dependent on uncertain energy supplies. Our national security depends on more than just our Armed Forces; it also rests on the strength of our economy, on our national will, and on the ability of the United States to carry out our foreign policy as a free and independent country."

I enjoyed the brief time (the cabinet meeting was just under two hours) with President Carter. Then just before Christmas I received a plastic encased package from the White House, containing the autographed book.

That fall I was president of the Iowa Daily Newspaper Association and Rosalynn Carter was invited to speak at our Cedar Rapids convention. At the start, I conducted a poor man's Phil Donahue talk show with Rosalind as our guest.

I brought the book for her to sign, which she did with a smile.

**First Lady Rosalind Carter, who spoke at the Cedar
Rapids Convention of the Iowa Daily Newspaper
Association in 1974 signing my book.**

Another guest to sign the book was Walter ("Fritz") Mondale
who had been our newspaper carrier in Elmore, Minnesota, in his
youth. He had delivered the Globe-Gazette, which I had published,
and I often invited him to engage in contests with our carriers. In

one contest, he tossed a rolled up newspaper and knocked down a framed picture from a wall to the delight of our carriers. Mondale became a lawyer, senator and, of course, vice president for Jimmy Carter. When he visited in 1974, I awarded him a bag pictured below.

Vice President Walter Mondale under President Carter was a former carrier for the *Mason City Globe-Gazette*.

**Interview of President Jimmy Carter by
me at the White House in 1978.**

In my final appraisal of Jimmy Carter, I have credited him with being an ethical president, who worked hard to improve relations between Arabs and Jews, earning him a Nobel Peace prize. However, in total, I would say he is a better past president than he was as a president. That was my opinion until he attended the funeral for a respected African-American woman and used the occasion to deride President George Bush. That was not an appropriate venue for that action. It reminded me too much of the Democratic "rally" at the funeral for Paul Wellstone when a Republican friend was heavily booed and ridiculed for attending Wellstone's calling hours. This undoubtedly hurt Walter Mondale's Democratic campaign as well. Proper respect should be given at funerals.

James E. Carter (October 1, 1924-) was our 39th president, serving from 1977-81, with Vice President Walter Mondale.

Chapter Eight

Ronald Reagan

Reagan: Intuition

Ronald Reagan had the uncanny knack for making judgments on "gut instincts" or intuition. Hugh Sidey, former presidential writer for *Time Magazine,* should be credited with describing Reagan's intuition. I met Sidey, formerly of Iowa, when I was in Iowa, too.

Most of Reagan's decisions received receptive responses. He was a great communicator and few could dislike him. His skills contributed to his high popularity standing of about 65 per cent as he left office. Regrettably Alzheimer's disease ravaged his body until his death at 94.

Ronald Reagan was the oldest (74) to be elected president in 1980. Somehow he escaped the threat of dying in office, which was said to plague those elected in years divisible by 20. So he did survive a would-be assassin's attack.

Probably the most charitable assessment of Reagan's talents was that he convinced Americans to believe in themselves.

When I was in Kewanee, Illinois, one of the leaders learned that a convincing speaker was to appear in Chicago to speak on behalf of Barry Goldwater in his campaign for president. That turned out to be Ronald Reagan, already a popular (and handsome) movie star. So about six of us boarded the Burlington Zephyr and rode into Chicago.

Reagan was a delight to hear, offering words of wit and (yes) solid conservative judgment. He was still, despite his age, a handsome lean figure with very little, if any, gray hair. Before his speech I went up to kneel before him at the head table to interview him. Reagan and I had a mutual friend, Don Herbert who played Mr. Wizard on television. Don also played opposite Nancy Reagan in a 1940 summer theater production when she was still Nancy Davis. Don Herbert and Ronald Reagan became friends when they both worked on the G.E. Theater during the 1950s. Don grew up in Kewanee and we both appeared in a college play together, since we both attended La Crosse State College. I'll describe more about Don in a later piece.

Not many people know that when Reagan was a lifeguard at Lowell Park Beach on the Rock River near Dixon, Illinois, he was credited with saving 77 lives. Some local folks claim he put a notch in a log every time he pulled a swimmer to safety. In fact, I learned that when he descended into Alzheimer's dementia, he forgot having served as president but remembered saving lives as a lifeguard.

He was born in Tampico, Illinois, and his family moved to Dixon when Reagan was nine. At North Dixon high school, he was busy with sports and dramatics, so busy, in fact, that Phyllis Landis supposedly did his book reports. The future president played the lead in his senior class play, which was, *Captain Applejack.* He had made his stage debut in *You and I* as a junior. In our days in Kewanee, Illinois, we often visited Tampico and Dixon.

Even though I had a very special fondness for Reagan, we reporters had planned to stay just long enough to catch the first of his speech and then take the train back to Kewanee. Reagan was so entertaining and dynamic that the group voted to remain for the total talk, miss the train, and rent a car to drive back to Kewanee. His self-deprecating humor endeared him to the audience and made him seem modest and natural, despite having been a leading movie star, long-time president of the Screen Actors Guild, famous anti-communist, GE Theater host, and leading political spokesman.

So when he was elected president, I applied for press credentials to his inauguration for me, my wife, and daughter Kathleen.

At his inaugural address on January 20, 1981, he described how the American government had grown so large that he intended to "reverse the growth of government." He stressed that "we will again be the exemplar of freedom and a beacon of hope for those who do not now have freedom." He added that "no arsenal is so formidable as the will and moral courage of free men and women."

For the first time ever, this inaugural was on the West Front of the Capital. Reagan noted the Washington monument and said, "He led America out of revolutionary victory into infant nationhood." He noted the "stately memorial" to Thomas Jefferson, and the "dignified columns" of the Lincoln Memorial. He then told us of a soldier in World War I who died under heavy artillery fire in France. On his body was a diary which read "My Pledge. America must win this war. Therefore, I will work, I will save, I will endure, I will fight cheerfully and do my utmost, as if the issue of the whole struggle depended on me alone." He ended by saying "With God's help, we can and will resolve the problems which now confront us."

His address was not only stirring but moments after he was sworn in, an elated announcement said that the American hostages held in Iran for 444 days had just been freed.

A kind photographer gave me another set of photo credentials and we were assigned to gala events in the Air and Space Museum. Our daughter, Kathleen Woody, formerly with the U.S. Interior and Justice departments and now with a financial consulting firm, attended the ball with us. She summed it up neatly by saying, "Geez, this is like going to the prom with your parents as chaperones."

The biggest treat was meeting John Warner and his wife, Elizabeth Taylor. We passed each other in a narrow gap between tables and Senator Warner greeted my wife, Betty. So I asked Elizabeth Taylor, coming next, if she couldn't greet me, too. I said, "That's no fair. Your husband just shook my wife's hand so I should get to shake yours." As my right hand searched for that one glorious handshake, she directed those marvelous eyes at me and I evaporated in goose-pimply mist. Still a beauty, she looked at me with those lavender eyes and I just wilted. She was as gorgeous as anyone I had ever seen. I would even have voted for her as president.

From all advance reports, I had been prepared to expect the movie queen to have blimped to Shelley Winters' proportions. But she looked lovely and quite trim.

Easily she was the star personality at the Air and Space Museum ball, which most Iowans attended. Sure, Robert Goulet, the singer, and Sen. Barry Goldwater, the ultimate conservative, were among the notables but all eyes were on Liz Taylor, except when that other movie star, Ronald Reagan, made his appearance.

By the way, I tried to talk Ronald Reagan into taking me to Europe (on the trip where he admonished the Russians to tear down the Berlin gates to Germany). He took my card with him, saying he had to go work out in the White House gym, but never got back to me about the trip.

To Gerald Moriarity
With best wishes,

Ronald Reagan

At Ronald Reagan's inauguration.

Here is my story of the 1981 inauguration for the *Globe-Gazette* in Mason City, Iowa, on Wednesday, January 21, 1981.

Inauguration Exciting, Suspenseful

By Jerry Moriarity, Globe-Gazette Publisher

The 1981 presidential inaugural, now history, surely dwarfs all previous spectacles and not only because of the cost—estimated roughly at more than $11 million.

It featured a unique blend of excitement, razzle-dazzle galas and balls as well as the cliff-hanging suspense over resolution of the American hostage issue.

Tuesday was supposed to have been Ronald Wilson Reagan's day as he became 40th president of the United States. He was denied complete dominance of the news because of the hostage issue.

But the Democratic leader he replaced, Jimmy Carter, was denied even more, despite feverish time-consuming efforts that occupied most of the waning hours of his term. President Carter was unable to savor his final moment of exaltation as the Iranians refused to approve the release of the hostages until Carter moved into the history books.

Perhaps it was this dichotomy that made the final day of celebration so unique and so great. We observed the triumph of the new and the sad frustration of the old, but somehow they came together in a feeling of compassion and unity.

Ronald Reagan took his oath of office at noon Tuesday and followed his acceptance with a promise "to act together in order to preserve tomorrow."

As he pointed to the monuments of patriots and heroes of the past, he asked Americans "to dream heroic dreams."

The former California governor and movie star called for an "era of national renewal" in his 15-minute address. His inauguration attracted more than 250,000 people to Tuesday's events, a total exceeded probably only by the Bicentennial observance of 1976.

Although scattered wrap-up activities were being held in various parts of the snow- and ice-swept District of Columbia today, officially the inauguration closed with eight formal balls Tuesday night and a number of unofficial balls.

When President Reagan and his wife Nancy appeared at the ball at the National Air and Space Museum—which most Iowans attended—U.S. Sen. Roger Jepsen and Gov. Robert Ray had their moment of glory on stage along with Elizabeth Taylor Warner, Robert Goulet and selected notables.

Reagan aroused cheers and applause, particularly when he said, "I refuse to refer to them (the Americans held in Iran) as hostages. I prefer to call them what they were, prisoners of war!"

The Iowa ball was indeed spectacular. There were three dancing areas with music furnished by the Houston Pops Orchestra, Sammy Kaye and Lionel Hampton.

Jepsen was host to a breakfast for Iowans this morning. Newly elected Sen. Charles Grassley has been observed at a number of events, and he was honored Sunday at a reception at the home of James Leech, Iowa congressman.

Leigh Curran and his family of Mason City have been seen at most of the events in Washington and he says he is enjoying every minute of it. He last attended an inauguration in 1972 when Richard Nixon was elected and Curran, then a state senator, was sent as an official delegate of that body.

We also have seen Pete Conroy, Mason Cityan working on the House Select Committee on Aging's sub-committee on human services here, who attended a reception for the 3rd District's new representative, Cooper Evens, R-Grundy Center.

* * *

Yes, my wife and I attended Reagan's inauguration and ball but I must confess some rather mundane memories. I am as patriotic as the next person. You can color me red. You can color me white. But you can't color me blue. And that's what I was for the opening January 1981 presidential inaugural ceremonies in Washington, D.C.

As Reagan pointed to the monuments of patriots and heroes of the past, he asked Americans "to dream heroic dreams."

The former California governor and movie star called for "an era of national renewal" in his 15-minute address. His inauguration attracted more than 200,000 people to the day's events, a total exceeded probably only by the Bicentennial observance of 1976.

My wife and I went to the Lincoln Memorial program and literally froze to death in the sub-freezing temperatures. However, it was beautiful, exciting, stimulating, and even invigorating. Hollywood would have been proud.

The program at the Lincoln Memorial was absolutely tremendous. It was truly an extravaganza of pageantry, fireworks, and patriotic music.

Efrem Zimbalist, Jr., movie star, was the host, but he was overshadowed by the Mormon Tabernacle Choir and, of course, the appearance of President Ronald Reagan and his wife, Nancy, and Vice President-elect and Mrs. George Bush.

However, this evening could hardly compare with Sunday's activities.

As we were preparing for a rather routine calendar of events, we met with U.S. Sen. Roger Jepsen in the lobby of his apartment building, the Fountains in Alexandria, Virginia. He invited us to join him at a buffet at the Georgetown home of Sen. Mark Hatfield of Oregon.

Jepsen prepared us (my wife and me) by saying, "Except for the president and vice president, you will probably never see so much of the power of the new administration condensed in such a small area."

And he was right. As we alighted from his car outside the residence, we were greeted by Sen. Richard Schweiker of Pennsylvania, who four years earlier had been a vice presidential nominee and now will become the new Secretary of Health and Human Resources.

As we moved up the steps to the Hatfield home, coming down toward us was Henry Kissinger, accompanied by his wife, Nancy. Jepsen introduced us as old friends.

Several steps past this point, as we entered the home, we met and were introduced to Sen. Hatfield, who commented that he had just heard the news that arrangements to release the Mid-east hostages had been completed. Naturally, I regretted that Kissinger had passed by before I had this information.

From that point on in the house, it was unreal. We were shoulder to shoulder in virtually every room of the four-story house. But in addition to meeting many of the dignitaries of the new Reagan administration we found time also to sample champagne and orange juice (mimosas) and the buffet.

The guest list read like a political who's who. Besides the many senators and their wives we met, just to name a few: Richard Allen, National Security Affairs Advisor; William Casey, new head of the Central Intelligence Agency; Jim Brady, press secretary to Reagan; Mike Deaver, who is deputy chief of staff to Reagan; Adm. Hayward, who was commander of the Navy and on the joint chiefs of staff; and Nancy Reynolds, who has been transition secretary to Nancy Reagan.

We left that stimulating environment by cab with the Jepsens, dropping them off for a family reunion while heading for the Iowa governor's reception at the Sheraton Washington Hotel. It's hard to believe that more people were at the governor's reception than live in most Iowa communities. More than 20,000 people elbowed their way through the huge hall for the reception.

We chatted for a time with Iowa Gov. Robert Ray. He was especially pleased to have heard about the expected release of the hostages. He was in about an eight-foot square booth and greeted many of the party faithful from Iowa as they came up to greet him and his wife.

The next day we went to the vice president's reception and later to a reception for Cooper Evens, new congressman from the third district. The major excitement of the night centered around the gala at which Johnny Carson was the master of ceremonies of a star-studded program assembled by Frank Sinatra.

A few of the class acts should have been reserved for TV's "Saturday Night Live." Rich Little's impersonations drew laughs, but, on second thought, a number commented that they reflected poor taste. It was more like a Dean Martin Roast.

As long as we mentioned that, we may as well say that our biggest disappointment was seeing a pathetic Dean Martin overdoing his "drunk act" so realistically that he spent most of the evening of the gala with his shaggy, once handsome head almost touching his chest. On the few feeble attempts he made to applaud other performers he couldn't even clap his hands together.

We have to give credit to ol' Blue Eyes—Frank Sinatra—for keeping Martin on the sidelines, although he was supposed to be one of the featured stars. Sinatra escorted Martin off the rehearsal stage in the afternoon and judiciously kept him off the gala's program that night.

But the others were great. They included Johnny Carson; Bob Hope, always a favorite; Charley Pride; Mel Tillis; Charlton Heston; Donny and Marie Osmond; Ethel Merman; Debbie Boone; Jimmy Stewart; Grace Bumbry; the U.S. Naval Academy Glee Club and, of course, Frank Sinatra himself, who still has magic.

Ronald Reagan's four-day inauguration undoubtedly will be the most expensive in history, not to the taxpayers, but to the people who have sponsored and supported it.

There are all kinds of gimmicks and memorabilia being sold and everywhere you find jars of jelly beans, Reagan favorites. Gads, we never nibbled on so many in our life. Jars filled with jelly beans were everywhere and not a peanut was in sight. Jimmy Carter, who left office, took his peanuts with him and the "in" tidbits for the Reaganites are jelly beans.

There is such an air of excitement and anticipation in Washington, people seem to be ready to welcome the new administration after the somewhat dreary days just being concluded. The District of Columbia could best be described as a happy zoo. The confusion was near chaotic. Traffic often was at a standstill because of the tremendous crowds. The scurrying for tickets was unbelievable. The governors' reception and vice president's bash attracted more than 20,000 each as did the gala.

Ronald Reagan's tremendous ability to laugh at himself is one of his legendary traits. When John Hinckley, Jr., shot him on March 30, 1981, he told Nancy, "Honey, I forgot to duck," borrowing prizefighter Jack Dempsey's great line. In January 1987, President Reagan was recovering from minor surgery for an enlarged prostate gland. He was quoted as saying, "My doctors told me this morning my blood pressure is down so low that I can start reading the newspapers."

Later I again got invited to the White House by Reagan, and got proof of how great Reagan was as a communicator. A press representative from Detroit wanted to sit at the president's table so he could tell Reagan how terrible conditions were in Detroit since Reagan got into office. I sat at the next table and saw how the fire in this fellow was doused and he sounded more like a little pussy cat.

To Gerald Moriarity
With best wishes,
Ronald Reagan

**President Reagan and Detroit representative who intended
to blame Detroit conditions on Reagan's presidency.**

Elizabeth Dole (Secretary of Transportation 1983-1987) was a guest at our table and I don't know if she noticed I turned over my dinner plate to check the model and design. Nancy, Reagan's wife, was in the tabloid news because she had (horror) purchased new tableware.

The next time in the White House was more interesting because my wife, Betty, again was invited along with another daughter, Mary Bridget.

On the stand were Reagan, Vice President George H. W. Bush and Pat Buchanan. Most of the questions were about Reagan's involvement in the Iran Contra scandal and it got rather uncomfortable at times.

Our daughter, Mary Bridget, was near the front lines and it was interesting to see a smiling George Bush (the elder) motioning to her to move over to get a better photo shot.

At last, Pat Buchanan, the press secretary, said that would be all the questions for today. But Reagan said he'd take one more and pointed to me.

He must have felt his decision was heaven-sent because I offered a powder puff question as it was near St. Patrick's Day and I figured he was sick of the Contra questioning.

So, with a smile, I asked, "How come an Irishman with the name of Reagan has a nickname of Dutch?"

I thought he would have kissed me if he could. So he explained in great detail how his mother originally planned to name him Donald and he would have preferred that. But I believe her sister named her son Donald so Mrs. Reagan switched to Ronald.

I wrote a newspaper piece for the Ottumwa Courier about this which follows.

How Did an Irishman by the Name of Reagan

Get the Nickname of Dutch?

By Jerry Moriarity

When Ronald Reagan was President, it was no secret that he was of Irish heritage. And proudly so, but how in the world did he get the unlikely appellation of "Dutch"?

Every year about this time as St. Patrick's Day draws nearer, my thoughts go back the more than 40 interviews I've had with the past 11 Presidents in the White House. And one in particular with Ronald Reagan stands out. In all, I had five interviews with him.

As editor and publisher of a number of Midwestern daily newspapers owned by Lee Enterprises, I was perplexed by this "Dutch" business. Of course, I wanted to know.

So, in March 1979, with an engraved invitation from the White House in my hand, I found the opportunity to ask Reagan THE question. Our Reagan visit came when I flew to Washington, D.C., to attend a governmental affairs conference, sponsored by the National Newspaper Association. For most of the convention-goers, the highlight was the White House reception hosted by President Reagan.

Patrick Buchanan, the White House director of communications, after a career as newspaper columnist and TV panelist, briefly introduced Reagan, whose robust stride carried him through the audience to the dais in the East Hall.

Most of Reagan's remarks, outside of the gentle humor he used frequently, concerned Nicaragua and his efforts to gain congressional support for aid to the Contras, opposing the Marxist Nicaraguan government.

He answered only two questions before Buchanan tried to terminate the session, which was turning rather heated, but Reagan spotted my raised hand and said, "I'll take one more question—from him"—meaning me.

With the overkill on Nicaragua, it appeared to be a good time to change the mood, so this roughly was my question: "Mr. President, I know you have many more pressing problems, such as the deficit and Nicaragua, but with St. Patrick's Day approaching, I wonder if you could explain how an Irishman by the name of Reagan got the nickname of Dutch?"

After the laughter subsided, Reagan obviously relished the chance to reply to a homey question that didn't try to sear his hide over some major issue. And the Great Communicator talked and talked and talked some more.

Oh, yes. How did he get the nickname? He said his father took his first look at him as a newborn baby and said, "He looks just like a big, fat Dutchman." The nickname took hold and persisted even through Reagan's days in Des Moines, as a sportscaster for WHO Radio.

Then really warming up to the name topic, Reagan indicated his mother actually wanted to name him Donald, but that her sister had a baby first and chose that name so Mrs. Reagan opted for Ronald. The president indicated that he would have preferred Donald.

Next the President's discussion meandered to his first days as an actor in Hollywood when studio officials wanted to change his name, even though Reagan was holding out to be known as Dutch Reagan. After the movie moguls suggested several unfavorable names for the future star, he quickly came around to the decision that his own name wasn't so bad after all.

When Reagan paused for breath and finally completed his comments, he stepped down from the platform and paused to shake my hand before heading toward the exit. Reagan probably wished he had more such creampuff questions from the regular hard-nosed press corps. He wasn't the first president to be proud of his Irish blood in his veins.

Most Irishmen and women still speak with pride about John Fitzgerald Kennedy. Andrew Jackson, Chester Arthur and William McKinley all had ancestors in County Antrim, Ireland. And Woodrow Wilson, Grover Cleveland, James K. Polk, Teddy Roosevelt, Harry Truman, and even Richard Nixon were among those with Irish backgrounds.

George Washington was not Irish, but he was a member of a St. Patrick's society. Once I asked George Herbert Bush (wearing a bright green tie) if he were Irish and he answered, "No, but I wish I were."

Although not all Irish are Democrats, this has reminded me of a story dating back to the 1938 congressional elections when John

Danaher became the first Irish Catholic ever elected to the U.S. Senate as a Republican.

As the tale goes, two old Irish women met on the street and one cried out, "Have y' heard? John Danaher has gone and become a Republican!"

"Begorrah!" her friend shouted back, "That kin't be true! I saw him at Mass just last Sunday."

* * *

I will close my discussion of Ronald Reagan with the interesting question: Did Nancy Reagan erase Tecumseh's Curse?

Most people remember or have heard of the situation in which presidents elected in 20-year cycles have died. At least until Ronald Reagan became president. Why was he spared?

Not long ago my son-in-law, who claims to be a fifth or sixth generation descendant of Tecumseh of the Shawnee tribe, provided interesting and varied information on this so-called curse.

What now is called Tecumseh's Curse actually was inspired by Tecumseh's brother, who was known as The Prophet, but whose name was Tenskwatawa. He was a respected preacher of the Shawnee people. Tecumseh was a heroic fighter, killed in a battle with U.S. forces, led by James Buchanan, later to become a U.S. president.

But The Prophet singled out William Harrison and said, "Harrison will not win this year to be the Great Chief, but he may the next time, but Harrison will die, I tell you. And when he dies you will remember my brother Tecumseh's death. You think that I have lost my powers. I who caused the sun to darken and Redmen to give up firewater. But I tell you Harrison will die. And after him every Great Chief chosen every 20 years thereafter will die. And when each one dies, let everyone remember the death of our people." The quotes were printed by astrologer Fred Bickum who picked them up from other sources.

Results of Tecumseh's Curse or The Prophet's Curse were rather convincing. It all started with Harrison, who was elected in 1840 and died of pneumonia. Abraham Lincoln was next. He was elected in 1860 and was assassinated. James Garfield, elected in 1880, also was assassinated.

William McKinley was assassinated in 1900 in his second term; and Warren Gamaliel Harding, elected in 1920 died in 1924 of a heart attack. Franklin Delano Roosevelt, whose third term started in 1940, died of a cerebral hemorrhage. John F. Kennedy, youngest president to die, was elected in 1960 and assassinated in 1963.

The change in Tecumseh's Curse occurred during Ronald Reagan's term when he was elected in 1980, but survived an assassination attempt.

Our son-in-law, Allan Gehn of Rock Island, Illinois, who lectures on Indian life and customs, has a theory about how the curse was broken or at least interrupted.

President Reagan's wife, Nancy, who was accused during her husband's term of being influenced by astrology and other signs, was freed of any consequences of Tecumseh's Curse, according to Alan's speculation. He believes the mental kinship by the curse's founder and the wife of President Reagan, Nancy, brought about interruption of the curse's impact.

Ah, well, time alone will tell.

On June 15, 1984, President Reagan wrote me a letter upon my retirement. He wrote:

Dear Mr. Moriarity:

Sen. Roger Jepson has kindly told me about your retirement as publisher of the Mason City, Iowa, *Globe-Gazette*. Nancy joins me in sending our warm congratulations.

Few shoulder greater responsibility and make more judgements than the professional newspaper journalist. In selecting news for coverage and the range of opinions presented to your readers, you provide a lifeline to your community and our nation. Your more than 43 years in that field is a remarkable milestone.

You are to be congratulated for your hard work and dedication which have earned the admiration of all who know you and for a career which has spanned much of this nation's history.

May your richly deserved retirement be healthy and happy. God bless you.

Sincerely,

Ronald Reagan

Ronald W. Reagan (February 6, 1911-June 4, 2004) was our 40th president, serving from 1981-89, with Vice President George H. Bush.

Chapter Nine

George Herbert Walker Bush

Bush—Coalitionist

George Herbert W. Bush had his finest hour when he mobilized the international coalition during the Gulf War. He wanted to be the AKAGA president—meaning A Kinder and Gentler America. But he was undone by giving in on his promise not to raise taxes.

I probably met George Herbert Bush under more titles than any other president. He was also UN delegate, ambassador to China, and chairman of the Republican party. This doesn't mean that I always got to interview him, but I did get to see him often.

First time I saw him, he was in charge of the Central Intelligence Agency (CIA). From there he moved up to vice president under Ronald Reagan and later became president on his own.

In fact, President Ronald Reagan visited Phoenix to promote the Bush-Quayle ticket and I was able to cover the story. Senators John McCain and Jon Kyl were seated behind the President in the picture I took.

**President Ronald Reagan promoted the Bush
-Quayleticket in 1992 in Phoenix, as did Senators
John McCain and Jon Kyl seated behind.**

I have transcripts from one talk in the White House when he mentioned my name several times to my surprise. Obviously, he could read my name on my tag as I sat in a front seat for his appearance.

When I first got in the room with him, I noticed he was wearing a bright green tie. I asked him if he had Irish blood in his veins, and he replied, "No, but I wish I did." He said he was going to a St. Patrick's party after the talk with Congressman Foley.

I also asked him a question about Mikhail Gorbachev, Russian leader who was having some trouble with his *glasnost* and *perestroika* efforts on restructuring Soviet political and economic policies.

But as he talked to the audience, he often referred his answers to "Jerry" to the surprise of some of my friends and to me, also. Here's the transcript of some of those comments:

Remarks and a Question-and-Answer Session at a White House Briefing for the Board of Directors of the National Newspaper Association March 15, 1990

Q. I'm Jerry Moriarity [Pine-Palm Publishing], from Minnesota and Arizona. I'd like to ask you: with all the power that's gravitating into the hands of Gorbachev while the Soviet world is collapsing about him, do you see any danger of a dictatorship evolving?

The President: No, because I think there's much less danger today given what they've done in their Parliament, or in their congressional side of things. They've come out of the totalitarianism of the past. They give the new President great power, but I don't see it as a threat, and I certainly don't see it as a threat at this juncture in history.

You know, I shifted our support going more like this: "We support reform and perestroika," to "We support Perestroika and reform, and we want to see Gorbachev succeed." I am convinced that one of the reasons we've had peaceful change in Eastern Europe is because of the approach that Gorbachev himself brought to bear on the problem. And I've consulted with him, had communications from him—one, for example, on the question of Germany—and I think he's a reasonable man.

So I'm not worried about the constitutional changes because as you look at the total picture inside the Soviet Union, you see an evolution that none of us would have believed possible 5 years ago or 3 or 2 in terms of democratic institutions. And I'm talking about the power in their Congress. They had a guy named Primakov who is the head of their Congress. And he was over here, and he came and told me—he said, "Well, I'm here to learn from the United States." And I said, "Mr. Primakov, you've come to the wrong guy in telling you what to do about the Congress. I'm not having too much luck. (Laughter).

But the very fact that he was here, you know, and in the spirit of very good well, getting—and I was only being semi-facetious there—but it's very different, Jerry, than it used to be. It's amazingly different. I dealt with these guys back in the United Nations, and I can't tell you how different it is in terms of self-criticism on their part or debate. When you have a difference you can do it agreeably. It doesn't have to be disagreeable like it was in the heart of the Cold War days. So I am not overly concerned."

That was quite an answer to my little question.

I snapped a picture of Bush holding his hands up. I joked that he wasn't showing the size of a fish he caught but perhaps the federal deficit so he could raise taxes, despite having said, "Read my lips; no new taxes."

**President George H. W. Bush March
15, 1990 at the White House.**

Sometimes I wonder how anyone can aspire to the presidency. The elder Bush often drew media heat. He was subjected to biased treatment by reporters and other-party politicians who called him a wimp. And yet he was the youngest Navy combat pilot in World War II.

And with Dan Quayle as his vice president, both were targets. On January 25, 1988, Dan Rather interviewed Bush about the Iran-contra imbroglio and kept trying to get Bush to say that he was involved in Iran-contra. Over and over again, Rather would ask Bush if he had prior knowledge and then interrupt him. This went on until Rather interrupted Bush for the last time, which ended the interview. A number of CBS affiliates called the Bush people to apologize for Rather's behavior. Bush may have won his skirmish with Dan Rather of CBS, but a Washington-based Center for the Media and Public Affairs found that in the two weeks following the "debate" reports were 75 per cent negative against Bush. Even so, Bush's strong reactions dispelled the notion that he was a wimp.

Attacks against Quayle were especially vicious and I wonder if Bush's fortunes would have improved if he had chosen someone like Colin Powell for the position. We'll never know. One of the attacks against Quayle was when Tom Brokaw was asking about his qualifications. Quayle stated that he had as much experience as John Kennedy in the Congress when he ran for president. Senator Lloyd Bentsen intervened saying, "I served with Jack Kennedy. I knew Jack Kennedy. Jack Kennedy was a friend of mine. You're no Jack Kennedy."

Quayle again came under fire when he helped judge a spelling bee. William Figuaroa, 12, spelled potato correctly, but Quayle, using a cue card, told him to add an "e" making it incorrect. That created a furor. But despite many unfavorable comments, President George H. Bush remained loyal to Dan and kept him on as vice president.

I always felt kindly toward Bush No. 1, who always acted as a gentleman. And I always remember how he tried to guide our daughter to a more advantageous spot to get Reagan's photo.

All recent U.S. presidents have had difficulty dealing with the press, particularly since Watergate when electronic and newspaper reporters have taken more liberties and have become more adversarial in their dealings.

It was interesting to learn on a trip to the Holy Land that Bush No. 1 did not favor the settlements being built on the Gaza strip by Israelis and he insisted that U.S. foreign aid not be used for that purpose, calling them an "obstacle to peace." Very surprising.

We often wonder how the former President Bush feels about the verbal and written abuse of his son, George W. Bush. The elder Bush did escape some of the mean-spirited comments because he actually had a decent administration and a war record. During World War II in 1944 his Navy plane was shot down over the Pacific island of Chi Chi Jima. That's when he made a parachute jump to save his life. It was interesting that he made another parachute jump on his 80th birthday and later he jumped for his sixth time in 2007, only months after he had hip replacement surgery.

So please don't call him a wimp.

George H. Bush (June 12, 1924-) was our 41st president, serving from 1989-93 with Vice President J. Danforth Quayle.

Chapter Ten

William Jefferson Clinton

Clinton: Resiliency

William J. Clinton remains remarkable in always being able to come back from adversity, including impeachment.

Truly he is one of the best communicators in recent history. Using his country lawyer skills he even could have walked away from Watergate. He could have been brilliant except for flaunting excesses in his personal life.

The past seems to keep coming back to haunt people. Clinton's predecessor vowed not to raise taxes and his "Read my lips" challenge did just that.

It made no difference if colleagues on both sides of the aisle urged him to change, but the public never forgot Bush was the one who changed and they elected Clinton.

At the time of his election, Clinton still was best remembered for giving one of the longest speeches at the last national Democratic convention.

But Clinton was a master of verbalizing his thoughts. We'll never know how a debate between him and Ronald Reagan would have turned out, although Reagan would have had less "baggage" to defend.

I had only two interviews with Clinton, both times in the White House. His wife, Hillary, was there for the first session and both of them autographed my invitation to the White House.

It was generally acknowledged that Hillary was smarter than a tree full of owls.

Despite his personal faults, there is much to admire about Bill Clinton.

When I met him in the White House on my second visit, I was able to size him up more. As we stood in line for a photograph, he seemed to be about two inches taller than my six feet. And he looked slim, fit and healthy, although this was before his heart surgery.

It is much too early to speculate about Bill Clinton's legacy. With recent economic downturns, many folks of both parties are heaping praise on Clinton for successes of his two terms as president, even though he was impeached. The "vent" columns of newspapers frequently say how well off people in the United States were when Clinton was president.

And he gets credit for not entering war with Iraq. But people forget some of his comments about the situation in the Mideast. On February 4, 1998, he said, "One way or another, we are determined to deny Iraq the capacity to develop weapons of mass destruction and the missiles to deliver them. That is our bottom line." On February 17, 1998, he said, "If Saddam rejects peace and we have to use force, our purpose is clear. We want to seriously diminish the threat posed by Iraq's weapons of mass destruction program." And, of course, it was one month after Clinton took office when a bomb exploded beneath the World Trade Center in New York City, killing five people and wounding many more. That same building(s) was leveled in 2001.

Despite these and similar comments by Hillary Clinton, Ted Kennedy, Sen. John Kerry, Al Gore and others, George W. Bush's detractors say he lied to the American people about the threat posed by Iraq and that we were taken to war unnecessarily.

By the way, it is interesting to note that despite rumors that Hillary was named for Sir Edmund Hillary, whom she met before he died, he became the first man to reach the top of Mount Everest in 1953, when Hillary was a mere six years old.

**President William Clinton with my wife
and me in the White House 1997.**

Clinton and the nation went through hell together when his dalliance with an intern came to light.

I did get to see how adept he was with explanations. When I first chatted with him, I asked a question and he gave a typical Democratic response. So I asked him for a Republican spin on my question and he gave a very acceptable answer and both parties could have been pleased.

Obviously he proved charming as well.

His indiscretions have been documented so I won't rehash them. Nonetheless his popularity with Democrats remains very high.

The nation should be pleased that after presidents are out of office, they tend to treat their former opponents more favorably. As examples, Carter became friendly with Gerald Ford and Clinton with George H. Bush.

His wife, Hillary, made a mighty good run for the presidential election of 2008, but has now been selected as Barack Obama's Secretary of State.

My wife and I took advantage of their White House hospitality and danced there to the music of a combo and not the Marine Corps unit that usually performs.

Both of the Clintons long will remain in the nation's memory book, so the chapter on the Clintons is not closed.

As a footnote to this information on Clinton, I will just add that when my wife and I were in Ballybunion, Ireland, searching for the graves of our grandparents, we were surprised to view an outstanding sculpture of Clinton prominently located near the heart of Ballybunion. He had pleased the locals by playing golf there so I took pictures of the sculpture and the plaque with the inscription below the statue.

I cannot leave my coverage of Bill Clinton without describing something about his perjury and impeachment over the affair with 22-year-old intern Monica Lewinsky. Despite Lewinsky's claim that they had sex nine times, when first accused, he said on January 26, 1998, "I did not have sexual relations with that woman." However, she turned over a blue dress to investigators, thereby proving her accusation with DNA evidence that could prove Clinton perjured himself.

Many believe his most famous speech was the "I Have Sinned" speech of September 11, 1998, when he admitted a sexual relationship with Lewinsky. Here are a few excerpts.

I was up rather late last night thinking about and praying about what I ought to say today. And rather unusual for me, I actually tried to write it down. So if you will forgive me, I will do my best to say what it is I want to say to you - and I may have to take my glasses out to read my own writing.

I don't think there is a fancy way to say that I have sinned. It is important to me that everybody who has been hurt know that the sorrow I feel is genuine: first and most important, my family; also my friends, my staff, my Cabinet, Monica Lewinsky and her family, and the American people. I have asked all for their forgiveness.

But I believe that to be forgiven, more than sorrow is required - at least two more things. First, genuine repentance - a determination to change and to repair breaches of my own making. I have repented. Second, what my bible calls a "'broken spirit'"; an understanding that I must have God's help to be the person that I want to be; a willingness to give the very forgiveness I seek; a renunciation of the pride and the anger which cloud judgment, lead people to excuse and compare and to blame and complain.

Now, what does all this mean for me and for us? First, I will instruct my lawyers to mount a vigorous defense, using all available appropriate arguments. But legal language must not obscure the fact that I have done wrong. Second, I will continue on the path of repentance, seeking pastoral support and that of other caring people so that they can hold me accountable for my own commitment. Third, I will intensify my efforts to lead our country and the world toward peace and freedom, prosperity and harmony, in the hope that with a broken spirit and a still strong heart I can be used for greater good, for we have many blessings and many challenges and so much work to do.

I thank you for being here. I ask you to share my prayer that God will search me and know my heart, try me and know my anxious thoughts, see if there is any hurtfulness in me, and lead me toward the life everlasting. I ask that God give me a clean heart, let me walk by faith and not sight.

Thank you. God bless you.

President Clinton was impeached by the House of Representatives on December 19, 1998, and acquitted by the Senate on February 12, 1999. The charges, perjury, and obstruction of justice arose from the Monica Lewinsky scandal and the Paula Jones lawsuit (whom he paid $850,000 for sexual harassment when he was Governor of Arkansas).

My final thought for now: Bill Clinton shows much promise, but he remains an enigma.

William J. Clinton, born August 19, 1946, was our 42nd president, serving from 1993-2001 with Vice President Al Gore.

Chapter Eleven

George Walker Bush

George W. Bush: Amiability (before Iraq) Legacy ??? (after Iraq)

If there ever was a U.S. president with an unknown legacy while in office, it is George W. Bush. The nation awaited his strengths after the divisive first-term election and he handled the 9/11 crisis well. Judgment after the start of the Iraq War will be unknown until long after he is out of office, if even then.

I have heard him speak twice, but only have met him once. I will be unable to appraise him until he leaves office.

Shortly after he took office, I had the opportunity to meet President Bush. This provided me with the opportunity to interview my 11th U.S. president in a row.

As a member of the National Newspaper Association, I was provided an invitation to meet the newly elected president in Washington, D.C. March 22, 2001. We didn't know what to expect. I flashed a picture of Bush as he was being introduced.

**President George W. Bush at the National
Newspaper Association March 22, 2001.**

Instead of the White House, our meeting was held in the Hyatt Regency Capitol Hill hotel in Washington, D.C. George Bush walked into the room after requesting the management not to play *Hail to the Chief.* He cordially greeted some folks along the main aisle.

After his introduction, he opened his speech with a discussion of the complicated budget. It was amazing to us, despite the talk's complexity, that we saw him glance down only once—on the budget section. The rest of his talk was virtually flawless.

We were all amazed. It was difficult for us to believe this was the man ridiculed almost every night by Dave Letterman and Jay Leno as a bumbling imbecile. Virtually everyone around us echoed the same comment, "We are amazed."

After deliberating on Bush's first positive aspect, I wrote down "amiability." Of course, that was before 9/11.

I wrote down a few of his sentences:

Remember, the context I come from, though, is not to do with what to do with the government's money, it's what to do with the people's money…I'm going to remember where it comes from. It comes from hardworking people. It comes from entrepreneurs, small business owners, hardworking folks who pay the bills for this government.

This country needs an education system that focuses on each child and says if you don't know what you're supposed to know, we're all going to come together to make sure you do early, before it's too late.

I am concerned about morale and the troops. So, we've increased the budget for better pay and better housing. The mission of the military must be focused, and the job of the Commander-in-Chief is to focus that mission.

Another priority is retirement systems of Americans. And so the budget I set up says the payroll taxes are only going to be spent on one thing, and that's Social Security—that the Congress won't be using the payroll taxes for other programs.

We double the Medicare budget in the budget I submitted to the United States Congress. The budget I submitted pays down $2 trillion of debt over a 10-year period of time. I also am aware that sometimes things don't go as planned. So in the budget we submitted, there's $1 trillion over 10 years for contingencies. And I'm asking Congress for a refund for the people.

America is, the harder you work, the easier the middle class ought to become, and the more money you get to keep. And by dropping the bottom rate and increasing the child credit, we make the code much more fair to people at the bottom end of the economic ladder.

It's important for our country to be a nation that honors—that respects other people's opinions. That's what democracy should be all about.

I hope—my hope of hopes is once my stay is through up here somebody says, well, you know, I think I might try to enter the public arena. I'd like to try to serve my country.

You may not agree with my budget but when it's all said and done, I think you will agree with how I conduct myself in public office.

By the way, I had my own presentation at the National Newspaper Conference in 2001 showing the pictures I had taken of the last eleven presidents.

Author's display at the National Newspaper Association in Washington, D.C. in March 2001.

The nation awaited Bush's strengths after the divisive first-term election. And he handled the 9/11 crisis well. He surprised the pollsters by winning re-election handily, despite massive dissent over the Iraq War.

For now it appears that his legacy will depend on the conclusion of the Mideast conflicts. If successful, he could be known as the "Liberation President."

But with the 2006 election of Democrats to positions of legislative authority this appears unlikely unless there is a dramatic reversal of fortune.

After his talk that March day in 2001, he strolled down the line, greeting well-wishers. I finally got to talk to him when Arnold Schwartz, managing editor of the Publishers Auxiliary, NNA newspaper, got room for me in the front line.

I mentioned that I had interviewed his dad three times (actually it was four) but this was my first opportunity to meet him.

He immediately responded with a laugh, saying "What took you so long?"

I remarked to myself, "This guy would be a good one to know."

I learned early in my career that presidents I've interviewed send you signed Christmas cards every year. The last that I received was from George and Laura Bush in 2007.

**Me holding a picture I took of President
George Walker Bush in 2007.**

I later heard him speak in St. Cloud, Minnesota, and it was interesting that the famous football coach of St. John's University at Collegeville, Minnesota, was there to speak on his behalf.

The coach, John Gagliardi, is the winningest football coach in the nation and two of our sons, Timothy and Joseph, played for him.

President Bush has been under attack since he launched his political career. Even his dad, the youngest naval combat pilot, shot down in World War II, came under attack by being called a "wimp," as I mentioned earlier.

George Walker Bush (most everyone recognizes the W in his name) has three major victories to his record. In Texas, he defeated the popular woman governor Ann Richards, to obtain prominence in Republican circles.

Then he was the winner in the contested race with Al Gore for the presidency, which will be argued for years.

Next he surprised pollsters in his second presidential campaign by winning re-election as president with a ton of votes, despite massive dissent over the Iraq War.

The dissent remains as the country still is divided over Iraq, despite Bush's nationwide appeal for a surge in combat military power. As I wrote, Bush's legacy will depend on the conclusion of Mideast conflicts if that day ever arrives.

Even though George W. Bush has a master's degree and is always ridiculed as a cartoon character, why did the opponents and comics (cartoonists included) never criticize Al Gore for dropping out of law school and even divinity school? Let the record show that George W is smarter than he is made out to be.

George Bush's legion of critics—and there are many—certainly knew how to go to his jugular when they truly bush-whacked him, even before he took office. If it would make Bush feel better, Truman had low ratings but he now is acclaimed as a fine president. Even Abraham Lincoln was ridiculed mercilessly, often characterized as a raging baboon. Yet today he is highly rated along with George Washington.

The trouble with Muslim nations didn't start with George Bush. As early as 1979 our embassy was taken over by Iran. The next year Americans were kidnapped in Lebanon. In 1983 many Marines were killed in Beirut; even the World Trade Center was bombed in the basement in 1993 as a prelude to the terrible aerial bombing later which leveled both towers with the loss of thousands. How patient should we be when Muslim fundamentalists vow to wipe us out? Should our answer be to continue to Bush-whack Bush?

One poll of about 1,000 persons that seldom (if ever) is quoted is the *USA Today* Gallup Poll in which George W. Bush has been voted the most admired man in the United States. This has been his sole honor in the poll for the sixth straight year. Hillary Clinton shared the honor among women. The poll was taken between December 14 and 16, 2007, and has a margin of sampling error of about three percentage points. The question as to the most admired man was worded as follows: "What man that you have heard or read about, living today in any part of the world, do you admire most?"

To where did most of Bush's detractors disappear? Yes, he has fallen some in the rankings over the last four years but he still captured the number one spot by the thousand people who were sampled.

George Bush also has a little known recognition. He is considered probably the stingiest president of modern times for doling out the smallest number of pardons. However, if the Democrats succeed in indicting all the Bush administration in the last year of rule, his pardon total may soar astronomically. But who would pardon him?

Everybody seems to acknowledge that George W. Bush's ratings as president are the lowest in 70 years since the Gallup Poll was started. But obviously few know or have forgotten that Bush also has the record for the highest approval rating in Gallup's history. This goes back to September 2001, days after the Twin Towers in New York were blown up by terrorists. Bush's record approval then was 90 percent but in April of 2008, the total had dwindled to 28 percent.

If ever this country needed to hear from their President, it was after the terrible attacks of September 11, 2001. Most people believe that President Bush rose formidably to the occasion with his address to the people nine days later. These excerpts may remind us of what George W. Bush told us in his finest hour when we needed him most.

In the normal course of events, Presidents come to this chamber to report on the state of the Union. Tonight, no such report is needed. It has already been delivered by the American people.

We have seen it in the courage of passengers, who rushed terrorists to save others on the ground--passengers like an exceptional man named Todd Beamer. And would you please help me to welcome his wife, Lisa Beamer, here tonight. We have seen the state of our Union in the endurance of rescuers, working past exhaustion. We've seen the unfurling of flags, the lighting of candles, the giving of blood, the saying of prayers—in English, Hebrew, and Arabic. We have seen the decency of a loving and giving people who have made the grief of strangers their own. My fellow citizens, for the last nine days, the entire world has seen for itself the state of our Union—and it is strong.

Tonight we are a country awakened to danger and called to defend freedom. Our grief has turned to anger, and anger to resolution. Whether we bring our enemies to justice, or bring justice to our enemies, justice will be done. I thank the Congress for its leadership at such an important time. All of America was touched on the evening of the tragedy to see Republicans and Democrats joined together on the steps of this Capitol, singing "God Bless America." And you did more than sing; you acted, by delivering 40 billion dollars to rebuild our communities and meet the needs of our military. And on behalf of the American people, I thank the world for its outpouring of support. America will never forget the sounds of our National Anthem playing at Buckingham Palace, on the streets of Paris, and at Berlin's Brandenburg Gate.

Americans have known surprise attacks but never before on thousands of civilians. All of this was brought upon us in a single day--and night fell on a different world, a world where freedom itself is under attack. Americans have many questions tonight. Americans are asking: Who attacked our country? The evidence we have gathered all points to a collection of loosely affiliated terrorist organizations known as al Qaeda. They are some of the murderers indicted for bombing American embassies in Tanzania and Kenya, and responsible for bombing the USS Cole. Al Qaeda is to terror what the mafia is to crime. But its goal is not making money; its goal is remaking the world and imposing its radical beliefs on people everywhere.

This group and its leader, a person named Osama bin Laden, are linked to many other organizations in different countries, including the Egyptian Islamic Jihad and the Islamic Movement of Uzbekistan. There are thousands of these terrorists in more than 60 countries. They are recruited from their own nations and neighborhoods and brought to camps in places like Afghanistan, where they are trained in the tactics of terror. They are sent back to their homes or sent to hide in countries around the world to plot evil and destruction.

And tonight, the United States of America makes the following demands on the Taliban: Deliver to United States authorities all the leaders of al Qaeda who hide in your land. Release all foreign nationals, including American citizens, you have unjustly imprisoned. Protect foreign journalists, diplomats, and aid workers in your country. Close immediately and permanently every terrorist training camp in Afghanistan, and hand over every terrorist, and every person in their support structure, to appropriate authorities. Give the United States full access to terrorist training camps, so we can make sure they are no longer operating. These demands are not open to negotiation or discussion. The Taliban must act, and act immediately. They will hand over the terrorists, or they will share in their fate.

Americans are asking, why do they hate us? They hate what they see right here in this chamber—a democratically elected government. Their leaders are self-appointed. They hate our freedoms—our freedom of religion, our freedom of speech, our freedom to vote and assemble and disagree with each other. They want to overthrow existing governments in many Muslim countries, such as Egypt, Saudi Arabia, and Jordan. They want to drive Israel out of the Middle East.

By sacrificing human life to serve their radical visions—by abandoning every value except the will to power—they follow in the path of fascism, Nazism, and totalitarianism. And they will follow that path all the way, to where it ends: in history's un-marked grave of discarded lies. Americans are asking: How will we fight and win this war? We will direct every resource at our command—every means of diplomacy, every tool of intelligence, every instrument of law enforcement, every financial influence, and every necessary weapon of war—to the disruption and to the defeat of the global terror network.

Now this war will not be like the war against Iraq a decade ago, with a decisive liberation of territory and a swift conclu-sion. Our response involves far more than instant retaliation and isolated strikes. Americans should not expect one battle, but a lengthy campaign, unlike any other we have ever seen. It may include dramatic strikes, visible on TV, and covert operations, secret even in success. We will starve terrorists of funding, turn them one against another, drive them from place to place, until there is no refuge or no rest. And we will pursue nations that provide aid or safe haven to terrorism. Every nation, in every re-gion, now has a decision to make. Either you are with us, or you are with the terrorists. From this day forward, any nation that continues to harbor or support terrorism will be regarded by the United States as a hostile regime.

Our nation has been put on notice: We're not immune from attack. We will take defensive measures against terrorism to pro-tect Americans. These efforts must be coordinated at the highest level. So tonight I announce the creation of a Cabinet-level posi-tion reporting directly to me—the Office of Homeland Security. And tonight I also announce a distinguished American to lead this effort, to strengthen American security: a military veteran, an effective governor, a true patriot, a trusted friend – Pennsyl-vania's Tom Ridge. He will lead, oversee, and coordinate a com-prehensive national strategy to safeguard our country against terrorism, and respond to any attacks that may come.

We ask every nation to join us. We will ask, and we will need, the help of police forces, intelligence services, and banking sys-tems around the world. The United States is grateful that many nations and many international organizations have already responded—with sympathy and with support.

Americans are asking: What is expected of us? I ask you to live your lives, and hug your children. I know many citizens have fears tonight, and I ask you to be calm and resolute, even in the face of a continuing threat. I ask you to uphold the values of America, and remember why so many have come here. We are in a fight for our principles, and our first responsibility is to live by them.

The thousands of FBI agents who are now at work in this investigation may need your cooperation, and I ask you to give it. I ask for your patience, with the delays and inconveniences that may accompany tighter security; and for your patience in what will be a long struggle. I ask your continued participation and confidence in the American economy. Terrorists attacked a symbol of American prosperity. They did not touch its source. America is successful because of the hard work, and creativity, and enterprise of our people. These were the true strengths of our economy before September 11th, and they are our strengths today. And, finally, please continue praying for the victims of terror and their families, for those in uniform, and for our great country. Prayer has comforted us in sorrow, and will help strengthen us for the journey ahead.

Each of us will remember what happened that day, and to whom it happened. We'll remember the moment the news came—where we were and what we were doing. Some will remember an image of a fire, or a story of rescue. Some will carry memories of a face and a voice gone forever.

I will not relent in waging this struggle for freedom and security for the American people. The course of this conflict is not known, yet its outcome is certain. Freedom and fear, justice and cruelty, have always been at war, and we know that God is not neutral between them.

Fellow citizens, we'll meet violence with patient justice—assured of the rightness of our cause, and confident of the victories to come. In all that lies before us, may God grant us wisdom, and may He watch over the United States of America. Thank you.

George W. H. Bush (July 6, 1946-) is our 43rd president, serving from 2001-08 with Vice President Richard Cheney.

Most everyone predicted Bush's conduct in the Iraqi War would be the major influence in the 2008 election. It was not as the economic troubles grew. The current recession had its start with the mortgage recession, which began with President Carter in the late 1970s.

Barack Obama, elected President in 2008, has been critical of industries moving to foreign countries but this began under President Clinton. Clinton's meeting on September 14, 1993, to empower the North Atlantic Free Trade Agreement (NAFTA) was intended to create a million jobs which never occurred.

Bush has been little recognized for his leadership in fighting AIDS by promoting delivery of life-saving medicine to more than two million people, a nice touch to his legacy.

Creating an Ideal President
By Jerry Moriarity

Harry S Truman—Feisty decisiveness, even directedness. He followed perhaps the most powerful president, Franklin D. Roosevelt. Truman was one of the more remarkable men to occupy the White House.

Dwight D. Eisenhower—Popularity, activism. This man of dignity gave America a breather after World War II. He was probably the most popular man in the world after the war. He is now being discovered by liberal and neo-conservatives as an activist.

John F. Kennedy—Humor and grace. The youngest president ever elected (41) and the youngest president to die. He possessed charm, youth and vigor. He was inspirational but a somewhat ineffective leader.

Lyndon B. Johnson—Power. He did what Kennedy could not do, enacting the Great Society. "He knew power like salmon know how to swim upstream"— George Reedy of Marquette University.

Richard M. Nixon—Astuteness in foreign affairs. He hurt himself more than he hurt the country during Watergate. He will be treated better after passing the scrubbing board of history.

Gerald Ford—Decency. He was the most decent individual to serve after Watergate. He was in a virtually no-win situation, pardoning Nixon.

Jimmy Carter—Ethical. Intelligent but insecure. He was the victim of the anti-Washington stand on which he ran. He turned out to be a mediocre president, but a great "past president."

Ronald Reagan—Intuition. He had the knack of making judgments based on "gut instincts." He articulated the direction in which he wanted the country to go.

George H. Bush—Coalitionist. His finest hour came during the Gulf War in mobilizing an international coalition, but he wanted to be president of AKAGA—A Kinder Gentler America. He was undone by giving in on a tax increase.

William J. Clinton—Resiliency. He remains remarkable in always being able to come back from adversity, including impeachment. Truly he is one of the best communicators in recent history. Using his country lawyer skills, he even could have walked away from Watergate. He could have been brilliant except for flaunting excesses of personal life.

George W. Bush—Amiability (before 9/11)…?? (after 9/11). The nation awaited his strengths after a divisive first-term election and he handled the 9/11 crisis well. He surprised pollsters by winning his re-election with the most votes in political history, despite massive dissent over the Iraq war. His legacy will depend on the conclusion of Mideast conflicts. If successful, he will be the "Liberation President."

PART TWO

Desired Interviews

If I could have interviewed anyone, dead or alive, my three ideal interviews would have been:

Mother Teresa
Muhammad
Copernicus

Those who heard me talk about the more than 40 interviews with the last eleven presidents always ask who your favorite president to interview was and who did you like best? That's like asking who my favorite grandchild is and I never answer that.

Seldom does anyone ask, "Is there someone else you would have liked to interview but never had the opportunity?"

Talking with and meeting world leaders have both made my career more interesting. However, so many journalists and others dwell upon the darker aspects of their subject's lives, and that is why I tried something different in creating an ideal president by taking the best qualities of each.

There are so many people I hoped to interview. Just think of the possibilities for interviews: Napoleon Bonaparte, Jesus Christ, Adolf Hitler, Attila the Hun, a leader of the Ming Dynasty in China, Peter the Great of Russia or even Ivan the Terrible. The possibilities are endless. They could include Alexander the Great who once controlled most of the known Western world.

There are the depths of the minds of famous people to explore— Julius Caesar, Lee Harvey Oswald, and Richard Nixon, each giving a slightly different spin. All of these are the reporter's dream interview. I will bet you could check with Richard Nixon if you had trouble finding the right word for a crossword puzzle, because he seemed so very intelligent except lacking in social skills in a large group of people. I used to call him the "evil genius."

One of the many reasons I disliked Lyndon Johnson was because of his vitriolic comments about others. He belittled Gerald Ford, our un-elected president, often saying that Ford played football too often without a helmet. Actually, Ford probably was the most athletic of the last eleven presidents I interviewed. Many others also ridiculed Ford when he pardoned Nixon for Watergate, but when Ford died in 2006; his action in pardoning Nixon was praised for ending the nightmare.

When people ask who my favorite president is, I always have a surprise for them. I like Zachary Taylor. In 1848, he refused the nomination letter from the Whigs because it arrived postage due. That's my kind of guy. Yep, he had told the post office not to deliver any letters with postage due because as a popular war general, he received many such. Therefore, the Whigs sent a second letter properly stamped and he opened it.

When asked who my favorite president is among those I've interviewed, I told one Danish reporter that there was a tie between two of my favorites: Harry Truman and Ronald Reagan. I told her, "I'd almost lean toward Reagan. He lifted the hopes of the American people." She wrote an article about me for the *West Valley View* in Litchfield Park, Arizona, on December 27, 2000. She flattered me no end when she called me in her article, "A Journalist with Presidential Credentials."

I have to confess that when I was first asked to compare President John Kennedy and President Bill Clinton, without thinking I said, "Kennedy—because he had better taste for women...Marilyn Monroe, Angie Dickinson..." My voice trailed off because of laughter, mostly from women, so when my speeches got dull I often threw that in. But let me return to Kennedy for a moment.

While I was attending mass in a Florida church years ago, I spotted Rose Kennedy in a pew midway down the aisle so I waited for most churchgoers to leave. When I walked up to her pew, I told her I had interviewed her son, the president John F. With hardly a pause, she told me, "He was not the one to be president. That was to be Joseph, who was killed in World War II." We barely got back to son Jack because she kept dwelling on Joe, the one who should have been president in her view.

Doesn't all this talk make us wonder if the other brothers would have been more qualified and how our world would be now? Because John F. Kennedy and I hit it off so well, many think he should be my favorite. Well, he is in some ways, socially for instance. Wouldn't it have been great to be on double dates with the likes of Marilyn Monroe and Angie Dickinson?

Surprisingly, I have narrowed my field of possible interviewees to three individuals and none of our readers would likely have guessed them. These three were chosen for different, but valid, reasons. My list includes one woman and two men. The choices may surprise you, but they are all renowned people that I would enjoy interviewing. They are listed in no special order.

Number 1: Mother Teresa:

She was one of the great women of our century, who dedicated her life to helping others and inspiring millions.

What could I possibly ask Mother Teresa? Many say she was a small nun with a big heart. And that certainly was true. She wasn't born into poverty by any means—just the opposite. She was born in Skopje, Macedonia, of Albanian origin. From the age of 12, she knew she wanted to be a missionary, so she joined the Loretto Sisters in Ireland, who sent her to India. She was appalled by the poverty and sought (and fought) to found her own Missionaries of Charity.

So great were her accomplishments, that she was moved closer to sainthood when Pope John Paul beatified her.

After speaking admiringly about her life, I probably would try to ask her, "How could you accomplish all the great things for the downtrodden that none of us could hope to do?"

Number 2: Muhammad:

With the perpetual unrest in the Midwest, I would have serious questions to raise with Muhammad, founder of the religion of Islam. If I were talking to Muhammad, who lived 570 to 632 A.D. in Mecca and Medina, I would question his principle that Islam is a religion of peace when radical fundamentalists have made the whole Arab world dangerous to non-believers.

"Would you try to restrain those who fault the so-called heathens and infidels and try to convert them by any means?" would be one of my questions.

"And why do Muslims interpret the *Koran (Qur'an)* as ordering them to subjugate and/or slay all 'infidels' who are non-Muslims? How can your followers persist in the belief that Islam is the religion of peace when that interpretation exists?"

Number 3: Copernicus:

I would welcome the opportunity to sit down with Nicolaus Copernicus and explore the marvelous mind of the Polish astronomer.

To Nicolaus Copernicus, who lived from 1473 to 1543 in Poland, I would ask, "How were you motivated to decide that the earth was not central to the universe when this was not common knowledge in your own time? What made you believe that the earth was not that important? How did you convince others of the correctness of your theory?"

What Others Have Said

For history buffs that came to listen to my talks about presidents, I sometimes included some questions and comments like the following:

Who had the shortest term in office? It was William Henry Harrison, who caught a cold and died 32 days after taking office.

Who never had a day of schooling in his life? That was Andrew Johnson, Lincoln's successor.

Under whose presidency was the most territory acquired by the U.S.? Of course, Thomas Jefferson acquired the Louisiana Territory.

What future president was expelled from college? James Buchanan was expelled from Dickinson College for disorderly conduct, but returned to graduate with honors.

Who said, "Honey, I forgot to duck." We all recall that it was Ronald Reagan after being shot by John Hinckley, Jr., in 1981.

Who said, "Government should do only those things the people cannot do for themselves." Ronald Reagan.

Who said, "I never give them hell. I just tell the truth and they think it is hell." Harry Truman.

Who said, "Let us never negotiate out of fear, but let us never fear to negotiate." John Kennedy.

Who said, "The lesson that most of us on this voyage [of life] never learn, but can never quite forget, is that to win is sometimes to lose?" Richard Nixon.

PART THREE

Other Famous People

Remembering FDR's Death

My first presidential experience came when my parents took me to see first Franklin Delano Roosevelt and next the 1928 presidential candidate, Al Smith.

I like to explain that my dad carried me in his arms, but truthfully I must have been 12 or 13 years old and it was the 1932 train that carried Roosevelt 8,000 miles. When the Burlington Zephyr pulled into the station, Roosevelt already was positioned in the center of the rear observation platform. His two sons were at his side. They had to be there to steady FDR, who suffered from polio, although his condition was not yet known to the general public.

Let's jump ahead to World War II, when I was an aerial and ground school instructor in the Air Force. It was at that time I developed an admiration for the Chinese people. When I received my wings virtually every member of my class was immediately sent overseas to Europe. I was one of only four retained to be an aerial and ground school instructor. Among my early assignments I was named to instruct three Chinese Nationalists, the two officers in the contingent and one student whose name I will never forget.

He was Yang Shou Tien, who I think could memorize logarithms in his head. He was brilliant, so remarkable that I had no problem always giving him excellent grades. So it was no surprise when he was selected as the outstanding Chinese cadet trained in the United States. Other nations had their own top cadets. Their reward?

The United States was to host a gigantic affair at Chanute Field, Rantoul, Illinois, for all the delegates going to San Francisco, where the groundwork was to be laid for the United Nations. So Yang Shou Tien and I were invited to participate. He and I were all suited up at the flight line in Deming, New Mexico, with parachutes in place.

We had just boarded the plane when a Chinese interpreter came running out to the flight line, waving his arms and shouting, "The flight has been cancelled."

He solemnly announced, "President Roosevelt just died."

We were both disappointed as we prepared to demonstrate the talent and skills of Yang Shou Teng before an international audience.

I was later recalled for duty in Southeast Asia because I was a radar navigator in B-29s. I was sent to Scott Field in St. Louis, but after four months there, the Air Force said it had enough B-29 volunteers and I wasn't needed.

I tried several times to locate Yang Shou Tien, even after China became a Communist nation. But I will always remember how we lost the chance to "star" in an international show at the time of Franklin Delano Roosevelt's death.

Many Interviews Were Interesting...

Having more than 40 interviews with the last 11 U.S. presidents and a robust list of other personalities, the question of favorite interviews always arises.

Either the question is asked, "Which president do you consider to be your favorite?" or "Which one would you like to interview again?" Very infrequently someone would venture, "If you could interview anyone, past or present, who would it be?"

Ah, that proves more exciting!

For that, I have three candidates under consideration, but first I will mention a few that have intrigued me.

Richard Nixon, one of the brightest, but most maligned leaders of our country, proved an interesting candidate for four or five interviews. Later, when Richard Nixon became president and embroiled in Watergate, I wrote his defense, which an Associated Press top editor said was the most widely reprinted editorial on Watergate, appearing in 573 newspapers across the country. So, Nixon would have been a good candidate for another interview, but through the ages he will be attacked or defended like Julius Caesar, Pontius Pilate or even Joan of Arc. He probably never will escape the ignominy.

Two of my favorite presidential interviews, however, were with Harry S Truman and John F. Kennedy. Neither, however, is on my list for future interviews.

Somehow I had one interview with Lyndon B. Johnson and that, in my opinion, was almost one too many. I never appreciated him because of his crude nature, although I must admit he was one of the most powerful men to inherit the presidency.

George Reedy, former UPI journalist and press secretary for Johnson after Pierre Salinger resigned, and later professor at Marquette University in Milwaukee said it best, "Johnson knew power the way a salmon knows how to swim upstream."

I personally resented his televised campaign ad against Barry Goldwater, showing a girl holding daisies and being blown up by a nuclear blast as what would happen if Goldwater were elected, but Johnson became a greater warmonger than Goldwater. Not surprisingly, I was one of the few to endorse Goldwater over Johnson, when I was publisher of the Star-Courier in Kewanee, Illinois.

Senator Barry Goldwater of Arizona, Mr. Conservative himself, was swamped by Lyndon Johnson in a race for the U.S. presidency, but he maintained a longtime image as a conservative politician. I invited him to speak to the Ex-PRESS Club in Sun City West, Arizona, which I helped form and was then president. Here we study one of his Kachina dolls. Goldwater was a marvelous photographer of Arizona and champion of its history.

Sen. Barry Goldwater with one of his Kachina dolls.

When I helped organize a club for ex-press people in Sun City West, Arizona, our first speaker was the father of Vice President Dan Quayle, newspaper publisher James Quayle. He had retired 24 days before he spoke to us in 1990, and told us it was none too soon. He described his career. He described the press lashings of his son with the story of how Dan Quayle "was no Jack Kennedy" and how the press accused Quayle of being dumber than a 12-year-old who could spell potato correctly. He thought he knew the publishing industry well but said it was shocking and painful to be on the receiving end of critical publicity campaigns about his own son. His son, Danforth, by the way, went on to write three books and has been a leader in investment and financial circles. For a time he was a distinguished visiting professor of international studies at Thunderbird American Graduate School of International Business in Arizona.

Sports interviews were many. Celebrities included Joe Louis, the famed Brown Bomber, Bronko Nagurski, famed Ukrainian football "fav"for Notre Dame and the Chicago Bears and wrestler, and plenty of baseball players such as Dizzy Dean and others. There was one boxer who made big time, but never won a title, just the adulation of stars in Hollywood. He was Hayden "Young Stuhley" Stuhlsatz of Kewanee, Illinois. He beat everyone he boxed but because the events were untitled, he was deprived of a crown. He called himself the "Uncrowned Middleweight Champion of the World."

He was virtually unbeatable but everyone concluded he took a dive for big money in a championship brawl. But he was glorified in most Hollywood and California newspapers. He even dated Lupe Velez. The Mexican American movie star also had a romance with Gary Cooper before marrying Johnny Weissmuller. She starred in *The Gaucho* with Douglas Fairbanks, Sr., Laurel and Hardy movies, and became famous in *Mexican Spitfire*.

Stuhlsatz returned to Kewanee with his handsome unmarked face, but he convinced a fellow in a tavern (The Dome) to take a mighty blow on his ear with the proper result—a cauliflower ear.

During my days as editor-publisher of the *Star-Courier* in Kewanee, he often brought dozens of his scrapbooks to my house, but I never copied the great stories written about him. He never missed church and always knelt in the front pew of Visitation Church with a red rose in his lapel. He had a fondness for drink and his life ended tragically when he stepped in front of a Burlington train. What an interesting character he was.

The Duke and Duchess of Windsor made an unusual interview when they came to the New Lisbon-Camp Douglas area in Wisconsin for a cranberry festival on October 2, 1941. Part of my interview was captured on film by the *Milwaukee Journal* as I ran down the railroad tracks to get in a last question as both smiled (perhaps laughed) at me as they leaned over the train's rear platform to answer me. I only have a rough copy of that picture left any more.

**Duke and Duchess of Windsor smiling
at me from a caboose in 1941.**

For those who may have forgotten, the duke abdicated his British throne December 10, 1936, in one of the great love stories of our time. He resigned as King Edward VIII to marry an American divorcee, Wallis Simpson. As head of the Church of England and as king, he could not marry a divorced woman.

I was fortunate enough to make the acquaintance of actor Cornel Wilde. I asked him to judge a beauty contest and we got on very well. He had just finished the movie *It Had to Be You* with Ginger Rogers in 1947.

The actor inscribed this picture "To Jerry Moriarity, my choice for Snow King. Cornel Wilde."

I invited John Glenn, first American to orbit the earth, and later a senator to be on my television channel when he was in town.

I can always say I helped astronaut John Glenn into his suit.

I was the first newspaperman in the United States to lease a channel on cable television for 24-hour news and advertising services. That was what I invited John Glenn to be on, among many other celebrities. This kind of station was so unique that it was written up numerous times and one of the articles describing it appears later.

Later in 1984, Glenn was a Democratic presidential candidate. While I was en route with Glenn to his speech in Iowa, he was asked whether Democratic candidate Rev. Jesse Jackson would affect him or candidate Walter Mondale. He answered, "It's too early to tell. I'm proud of my own civil rights record and I'm not running off with this. I'm competing for every single vote in the country, whether they be Hispanic, white or black."

Glenn called Jackson an "able and articulate leader who will bring attention to the concerns of many people." He said, "Jackson's candidacy will add to the campaign rather than detract."

Bronko Nagurski:
Sports Legend

I wrote this story about him which was published February 18, 1999.

Greed Deprives Youth of Truly Great Heroes

Light years ago, when many of us mere mortals were just kids, we were blessed with heroes. I had at least three.

Of course, an obvious hero was Charles (Lucky Lindy) Lindbergh, who captured the heart of the nation with his solo flight across the Atlantic.

As a sports-minded youngster, I thrilled when reading newspaper accounts of the dazzling exploits of Red Grange, No. 77, of football fame. But more about him later.

However, the real man among men was Bronko Nagurski. He was bonafide! He was a dynamic battering ram for the University of Minnesota's Golden Gophers and later a legendary star of the Chicago Bears, a teammate of Red Grange.

We're pleased, just as that gentle giant would be, were he still alive, to see that he was honored on John Madden's All-Millennium team.

We met when he had just taken a sabbatical from football to become a professional wrestler. At that time, I was just a high school or early college student covering sports and other news for the *La Crosse (Wisconsin) Tribune*.

Perhaps because I always considered pro wrestling a farce and that the stories belonged on the entertainment pages, the editors seemed to take delight in having me cover most wrestling and boxing matches.

Sure, it was fun. I got to watch Andre the Giant, Joe Louis, one of the greatest champs of all, and even Mildred Burke, the "champeen" women's wrestler, who had more diamond rings on her fingers than I had coins in my pocket. She even autographed a somewhat glamorous photo for me.

But the Bronk was legitimate. A match I'll never forget was held in the old Avalon ballroom in La Crosse, sometime in the pre-war years.

At ringside, I marveled at Nagurski's massive body. One of his thighs had a huge bump, almost like a tumor, probably from his destructive ways on the football field. His huge neck, some said it was size 19, seemed larger than my waist. And his hands looked like baseball catcher's mitts.

His match with a younger opponent was exciting and devoid of the gymnastic shenanigans of members of the present-day "rasslin" fraternity.

Suddenly the opponent caught Nagurski by surprise with an unexpected body blow. The Bronk stood there a moment as his fury built. He crossed the ring in a flash and threw a vicious block into his foe, which almost knocked him out. The message was clear: Don't ever try that again!

After the match, a few of us went to one of the watering holes on Third Street. At that time, La Crosse, a Mississippi River town, had more taverns than St. Paul. I was there with Nagurski, Andy Skaff, the promoter, Jim Leinlokken of the *Tribune* staff and one or two others.

Now I have no recollection of what our conversation was about, but this hero of mine was one of the nicest, kindest people you'd ever want to meet. Not in a dark alley, of course.

My most memorable recollection? They brought Nagurski six hamburgers. He engulfed them in his massive hands and took no more than one or two bites as he devoured each of them.

Now briefly back to Red Grange who played in the same Bears backfield with the Bronko in the 1930s. La Crosse had a professional football team, the Lagers, playing against St. Louis, Decatur and others, some of which became big names in the NFL.

Bill Scanlan and I usually went to those games. And we always ran to see who could sit in seat 77 (Grange's number).

We had some great heroes in our youth, such as Nagurski and Grange. Somehow you get the feeling that some of our present-day youths have been somewhat deprived in an age of greed.

Harold Stassen—"Boy Wonder" to "Biggest Loser"

From "Boy Wonder" to Don Quixote of politics covers the lengthy career of Harold Stassen, part of the interesting fabric in American politics. Stassen died of natural causes in Bloomington, Minnesota, in 2001 at the age of 93.

Just think, it was seemingly light years ago—actually 1948—when as the state editor of the *La Crosse Tribune* in Wisconsin, I covered the presidential campaign, which eventually returned Harry S Truman to the White House. Yes, I'm going to spell Harry's middle name S instead of it having a period like a middle initial.

Up until that time, Stassen had an illustrious career. In 1938 he was elected to the first of his three terms as governor of Minnesota as a Republican and later served one term as governor of Pennsylvania. He appeared destined for great accomplishments.

He resigned in April of 1943 to join the Navy and he served nobly as an officer in World War II.

Franklin Delano Roosevelt, a Democrat, was impressed with this Minnesotan, and appointed him as a leading delegate to the San Francisco convention, designed to form the United Nations charter.

Stassen's career bloomed as he turned to presidential politics. His first race for the Republican nomination for president was in 1948 when he challenged Thomas Dewey for the GOP nomination. Dewey defeated Stassen in the primary and eventually lost to Harry Truman.

I covered several of Stassen's appearances in his first campaign. He appeared before an overflow audience in the Fifth Avenue Theater in La Crosse and I was impressed with how he handled questions from the audience.

He'd say, "There are five reasons" and he'd spell them out in order, one, two, three, four, and five without a pause except for applause.

Later, for some surprising reason, I was invited by the major radio station in La Crosse, then known as WKBH, to interview him on an evening newscast. Again, he had a flawless performance.

After his loss to Dewey, he became president of the University of Pennsylvania for four years—or until the presidential bug bit him again.

And, oh, how it bit him—a total of nine times—in 1948, 1952, 1964, 1968, 1976, 1980, 1984, 1988, and 1992.

It was fortunate that he did not have to contend with the biting humor or satire of Jay Leno or David Letterman, although his campaigns had become lessons in futility.

For some reason in later years, Stassen had covered his thinning hair with an ill-fitting hairpiece, which looked totally out of place.

All these losing campaigns appeared to be almost tragic and they detracted from what had been such a promising career. He did, however, serve as the Dakota County District Attorney in Minnesota and ran for Mayor of Philadelphia but was defeated. As president of the American Baptist Convention, he joined Martin Luther King for a march on Washington, D.C., in 1963.

Although Stassen had spent his last few years in a retirement center in Bloomington, Minnesota, one of his associates told us that he remained an amazing and able personality, who often took two steps at a time as he proceeded upstairs.

Stassen used up all nine of his political lives, but remained an interesting figure who contended that he had a winning life, even in defeat.

Wiretaps and the Press

All recent U.S. presidents have had difficulty dealing with the press, particularly since Watergate when electronic and newspaper reporters have taken more liberties and have become more adversarial in their dealings. Sometimes I feel that the laws of this country give the press more power than the president of the United States.

Through the years while serving as an executive of Lee Enterprise's newspapers in Wisconsin, Illinois, and Iowa, I arrived at two general conclusions. First, an adversarial press means a presidency in hostage. Second, each president becomes a reflection of the period he serves. Some win or lose wars, some are elected to bring calm after tumult, and others move innocuously along with varying results. But with all the scrutiny, one wonders how any president keeps from going off the deep end.

There have been deliberate distortions of information by reporters in articles lacking objectivity and becoming personalized opinion pieces masquerading as objective news stories.

TV reporters too often act like commentators. Unlike politicians, they were never elected by the public. Many have become arrogant second-guessers and worse, crepe hangers giving the public the worst take on anyone and any situation.

Wiretaps or monitors by Presidents Roosevelt, Eisenhower, Kennedy and Johnson were ignored by the media, and the public was led to believe that President Nixon was the only one who ever used electronic devices. He was an amateur compared to Johnson. Reporters did everything that Nixon was accused of doing, involving electronic surveillance and bugging phones.

Several examples come to mind in this report on what Thomas Jefferson called the "splendid misery" of the presidency. At one time during the early days of Reagan's term of office, the *Columbia Journalism Review(CJR)*, the so-called press watchdog, attacked the media for being "soft" on Reagan. C. T. Hanson, editor of the *CJR* wrote, "The White House Press served with unusual frequency during Reagan's first two years as a kind of *Pravda* of the Potomac, a conduit for White House utterances and official image mongering intended to sell Reaganomics." But later a team of social scientists analyzed all network news of Reagan on TV, and found that he was treated favorably with but 400 words out of 8,800.

Wiretaps and monitoring of telephone calls and other sources isn't unusual in the White House. Franklin Roosevelt had Stephen Early sit in a lower level room below Roosevelt's radio room for that purpose. Early was the first "press secretary" for a president, and even served in that capacity for President Harry Truman after Truman's close friend, Charlie Ross, died.

J. Edgar Hoover brought Truman some FBI phone taps made by Roosevelt, which had to do with sexual liaisons. Harry said he had no time for such foolishness and didn't authorize it. He wrote in his diary during the first month of the presidency, "We want no Gestapo or secret police. The FBI is tending in that direction. They are dabbling in sex-life scandals and plain blackmail. This must stop."

John F. Kennedy and Lyndon Johnson used the devices. Kennedy was involved with the twice-married Danish woman Inga Arvad when he was in World War II from 1941 to 1944. The FBI suspected she was a spy and bugged her apartment. Their tapes caught John in sexual adventures with her. These tapes gave J. Edgar Hoover, Director of the FBI, something to hold over Kennedy's head when he became president.

Doesn't anyone remember how Johnson gloried in his wiretaps, especially when he was able to check on the exploits of Martin Luther King? It certainly was no secret how Johnson delighted other politicians when he shared facts about that prominent person's night life. Where were the protests then? Sexual adventures of Kennedy and Johnson were ignored, but reports of one joke by Earl Butz, Secretary of Agriculture, brought him down. The October 18, 1976, issue of *Time Magazine* reported the comment when Butz was asked why the party of Lincoln was unable to attract more blacks. Butz said that "the only thing the coloreds are looking for in life are tight pussy, loose shoes, and a warm place to shit."

In fact, Johnson lectured Nixon to keep the wiretaps for future use by historians, but this in part led to Watergate. Many had the impression that Nixon was the only one to make recordings of the conversations by guests in the White House.

Even Walter Cronkite, called "the most trusted man in America," used recording devices, sneaking cables—both oral and video—into rooms where the press was barred. However, he is now one of a bipartisan group that is urging the cancellation of wiretaps by the National Security Agency (NSA). In 2007, the group called The Liberty and Security Committee of the Constitution Project went on record saying that the NSA's warrantless surveillance program is illegal. Walter Cronkite was busy getting his point across to someone at the National Press Club in Washington, D.C. in 2003 honoring Tom Brokaw.

Wiretaps can be valuable, especially when checking on possible terrorist activity. Protests often will be leveled that rights of individuals would be invaded, but they can be invaluable in determining guilt. But I have always felt that responsibility and accountability were major ingredients of journalism, along with a sense of decency. Now there's too much of a double standard. Editorial comments belong on the editorial page. Good journalists want it that way; the public wants and deserves to have it that way. Self-government and freedom of the press should be cherished in this nation, but there should also be freedom from abuses.

The Walter Cronkite School of Journalism at Arizona State University offers annual awards for the best journalist in the United States. Cronkite awarded Tom Brokaw the 2006 winner and Jane Pauley was the winner in 2007.

Self-government brings to mind a humorous exchange between Howard Cosell and George Will on television some years ago when media attention was focused on the Super Bowl. Cosell asked Will what it all meant. Will cooly replied, "It means that the United States is not yet ready for self-government."

Let us hope that no similar observation, humorous or otherwise, arises in regard to freedom of the press.

On that 2003 trip to Washington, D.C. for the National Press Club, Betty and I visited the White House and were photographed in front of a beautiful painting of Jacqueline Kennedy. We learned on that visit that Nixon's portrait was moved half way up the stairway to the second floor. High cost of infamy!

**Betty and Jerry Moriarity in front of a painting
of Jacqueline Kennedy at the White House.**

Another Memorable Interview: Sen. Joseph McCarthy

One of the unfortunate characters of the Truman-Eisenhower-Kennedy era still resonates. I got acquainted with Joseph McCarthy just before his senatorial career; in fact, I had to introduce him to people in western Wisconsin before his reputation was tarnished. His later tactics were labeled McCarthyism as an opponent of communists.

It started when the editor of the *La Crosse Tribune* assigned me to meet McCarthy and accompany several political dignitaries as they toured western Wisconsin. The editor, Roy Bangsberg, and I went to the Hotel Stoddard to meet McCarthy and the county Republican chairman. Several others showed up, but quickly said they had conflicts so that left the senatorial candidate and me to tour the area. It was natural for me because I was state editor of the *Trib* at the time and often traveled through western Wisconsin, southeastern Minnesota, and northeastern Iowa.

Honestly, it was a great trip and McCarthy was always a gentleman as he met voters in various towns. A few of his detractors tried to belittle him as "Tailgunner Joe" for claiming an injury as a Marine in World War II. But too many of them underestimated him as he toppled the La Follette dynasty in Wisconsin and was elected U.S. senator.

McCarthy gave the impression of being a kindly fighter for causes and he wore a dark beard which belied the kinder impression he offered. As a postscript, when I was active in the Wisconsin Junior Chamber of Commerce, I was asked to introduce him at a state convention. I even got to present him with a special gavel.

**Sen. Joseph McCarthy in Appleton, Wisconsin, where
I presented him with a special gavel in 1952.**

After he started to talk, I lit up a Dutchmaster President cigar, which probably cost 20 or 25 cents, which was the top of the class for me. But during his talk, he reached over, plucked the cigar out of my mouth, and dunked it in my coffee cup to the laughter and cheers of the audience. He promised he would send me a box of special cigars, but of course, he never did. His raspy voice apparently could not tolerate cigar smoke.

He is still considered a villain for his attacks on communists in the government. The most vicious attacks on him started on February 9, 1950, when he said there were 205 communists working in the State Department.

In later years, one writer asked, "He had no shame, but was he right?" Even now, some of the former employees of the State Department admit he was not completely wrong, but after he was censured by the Senate in 1954, he turned to excessive drinking and died.

His reputation probably never will be cleansed, but some disclosures indicate that there were influential communists in our government around 1944.

Later disclosures revealed that Soviet agents communicated with the Russian government and indicated that more than 100 Soviet agents had infiltrated the State, Justice, War and Treasury departments in the United States as well as the Office of Strategic Services (OSS). This was revealed through examination of cables sent to Russia. These cables provided evidence that American communists spied for the Soviets.

Alger Hiss and the Rosenbergs were defended vigorously in the States and McCarthy was assailed bitterly and viciously so that McCarthyism remains indelibly marked as evil personified. "McCarthyism" has a longer shelf life than he did.

I might just add that as the following letter explains, Joe died still owing me a box of good cigars and a case of champagne.

TENTH JUDICIAL CIRCUIT
LANGLADE, OUTAGAMIE AND
SHAWANO COUNTIES

MOTION DAYS
APPLETON: 1 P. M. ON EVERY DAY
THAT COURT IS IN APPLETON
ANTIGO: 1ST AND 3RD MONDAYS
10:00 A. M.
SHAWANO: 1ST AND 3RD MONDAYS
EVERY MONTH
2:00 P. M.

Circuit Court Chambers

JOSEPH R. McCARTHY, Judge

Appleton, Wisconsin

June 18, 1946

Mr. Jerry Moriarity
c/o LaCrosse Tribune

Dear Jerry:

Just a note to thank you again for
"taking me around" last week. I really appreciated
the contacts we made, and also the excellent write-
ups you were responsible for.

Keep up the good work, Jerry, and after
August 13th, I'll drop over with a case of well-
deserved champagne.

Seriously, I shall probably see you
again in the near future when I am back in that
part of the state, and shall certainly contact
you at that time. In the meantime, thanks again,
and good luck.

Very sincerely,

Joe McCarthy

JRMc:F

Sen. Joseph McCarthy's 1946 promise of champagne.

He Had a Chest Full of Medals:
Haile Selassie

A strange interview took place one day in 1955 in Rochester, Minnesota, where Haile Selassie of Ethiopia came for a visit, but chiefly to have a medical examination at the Mayo Clinic.

The tiny emperor was weighed down with a great number of medals.

The Allies in World War II liberated Ethiopia from Benito Mussolini's Italian forces. Selassie had made a world-wide appeal when Italian forces threatened to take over his country.

How I wish I had been more knowledgeable about Haile Selassie when I met him at Mayo Clinic.

Selassie became a powerhouse in Africa. It was interesting to note that he claimed to be a direct descendant of the Queen of Sheba and King Solomon of ancient Israel. For that matter, Saddam Hussein, illegitimate son of an Iraqi thief, tried to claim that he was a direct descendant of Muhammad.

Selassie had a chest full of medals as he claimed to be the Conquering Lion of the Tribe of Judah, Elect of God, King of Kings of Ethiopia, Lord of Lords, and dozens of other titles. Under him, Ethiopia had become a charter member of the United Nations.

But surprisingly, he was a Coptic Christian, opposed to the Islamic religion and he aligned Ethiopia with the West in Christian beliefs.

He finally was deposed by a Communist government in 1974 and died a year later under suspicious circumstances, many believing that he was suffocated by an assassin with a pillow. His body remained undiscovered for twenty years.

The only reminder I have of that 1955 meeting is a photograph taken by Don Swenson of Selassie and me but my interview notes have vanished, probably from the glare of his medals. While he was at Mayo Clinic, Phyllis Halverson, president of the University of Minnesota Nursing Association, presented him with a certificate to commemorate his deceased daughter, Princess Tshai's role as a nurse. The certificate represented a donation of nursing books to be used by nursing students in Ethiopia.

Haile Selassie, king of Ethiopia, speaking with me in 1955 during a medical visit to Mayo Clinic in Rochester, Minnesota. (Photo by Don Swenson)

Interviewing Errol Flynn:
Doing What Chicago Could Not!

It isn't often that one gets to interview Robin Hood, General George Custer, Captain Blood and Gentleman Jim (Corbett) at the same time. But I did one snowy night in La Crosse, Wisconsin.

I was just a cub reporter on the news staff of the *La Crosse Tribune* when an urgent call came into the office from a harried staffer of the *Chicago Sun-Times*. Errol Flynn, a screen idol of great proportions, had breezed through the Windy City, but none of the celebrity-hungry writers and photographers got close to him. He eluded them all.

One of the editors took a chance and thought he could be heading to La Crosse and, if he did stop there, perhaps someone from our paper could ask him a few questions.

Roy Bangsberg, our editor, thought this could be a possibility and assigned me to take a camera and wait at the Burlington train station, just in case. I was given a list of somewhat nasty questions to ask and also check out if he were traveling with several of the opposite sex, so typical of him.

As I waited in the severe cold in a foot of snow, two swell-dressed females stepped down from one of the cars. I recognized one as Rita George of La Crosse and the other looked like Doris Duke, a fabulously rich woman. But no Errol Flynn! (Doris Duke became the richest woman in the world when her tobacco and energy magnate father died, and was courted by gold-digger Errol Flynn.)

However, I waited until the train was just set to depart and this handsome person peeked around the door corner, ostensibly to see if the coast were clear. It wasn't because I was there all by myself.

Finally, he lightly stepped from the train and was confronted by me. One of his admirers had described him as being "wickedly handsome" and he was.

I started asking some of the questions the Chicago press had offered and some were embarrassing as they touched on his sexploits, which apparently were many.

Abruptly, he interrupted by asking, "Who in the hell wants to know, some #%&* bastard in Chicago?" I meekly responded, "Yes," and then asked him to pose for a picture.

First he said no, but I persisted and finally, he grandly stated, "All right, BOYS, just one." He must not have recognized that I was just one "Boy." But I got the photo, which showed him to be just as handsome as ever. He wore a fashionable cashmere coat and brown hat at a rakish angle.

Even from my perspective, I could understand how few women (if any) could resist his charms and magnetism.

The Chicago press did get the report on his "apprehension" in La Crosse and they made a major play of him being interviewed in Wisconsin after eluding the big city press.

At that time, La Crosse had its Snow Bowl for skiers in the Coulee Region bluffs and I headed out there the next day. But Errol Flynn and his two friends got there before me.

That week, John D. (Pink) Rice, editor of the *Sparta Herald*, a nearby weekly, wrote a hilarious column about how Errol Flynn was a better skier than this Jerry Moriarity of the *Trib*.

Pink was a good friend and competitor, wrote an interesting weekly column, and later was named to the Wisconsin Board of Regents.

But getting back to Errol Flynn, he was born in Hobart, Tasmania in Australia but his father eventually taught biology in a university in Australia and possibly later in Belfast, Ireland. Flynn claimed to have fought for Australia on its Olympic boxing team. He made other claims, such as being a member of a royal Irish family. True or not, he was a marvelous physical specimen, a quick master of his movie lines, a skilled swordsman and yachtsman.

In a 1980 book, author Charles Higham claimed that Errol Leslie Thomson Flynn fabricated much of his background and even was a Nazi spy, which other writers dispute. It was no secret that he favored Northern Ireland in its fight for independence from Great Britain and received help from Germany. It appears that his mother's side was descended from Fletcher Christian of *HMS Bounty* fame.

But to most men he remains "Robin Hood" and to women he remains a handsome Lothario, a bonafide Don Juan. He was accused in three statutory rape cases and gave rise to the phrase "in like Flynn."

To me he was the object of an interview in which I was almost too embarrassed to ask the "Chicago" question.

Meeting a Music Genius: Meredith Willson

One of the joys of being promoted to a number of daily newspaper assignments came when I became publisher of the Globe-Gazette in Mason City, Iowa. Because it was there that I became acquainted with a true musical genius, Meredith Willson.

Within the late years of his life, I had three great interviews with him in Mason City where he was born and to which he gave the official title of "River City." That title comes from his famous *The Music Man*, the story of a bandleader who tried to convince the folks in this town to outfit a band.

Even to this day, when I hear the stirring notes of the assembled band marching in glory, I get chills. I did not get to see the original production in Mason City, but I have viewed dozens of televised reproductions and stage re-enactments, some of which were wildly spectacular.

Willson's full name is Robert Meredith Reiniger. As a flute and piccolo player, he made musical inroads in New York and even for the John Philip Sousa band and New York Philharmonic orchestra conducted by Arturo Toscanini before becoming musical director for the NBC radio network.

The Music Man was probably his most famous work as he won the Tony award and title of "Showman of the Year." But he also was famous for *The Unsinkable Molly Brown* made into a 1964 movie with Debbie Reynolds as the *Titanic* survivor. He wrote many famous songs such as "It's Beginning to Look a Lot Like Christmas," "Gary Indiana," "May the Good Lord Bless and Keep You," sung by Kate Smith, and "Till There Was You," made famous by the Beatles in 1963.

During John Kennedy's presidency, he wrote "Go You Chicken Fat, Go" for the national youth fitness program. He had youngsters moving through exercises and activities at a frantic pace, led by Robert Preston who starred in *The Music Man.*

During one of my interviews, I asked him if he would sign an autograph for our youngest son, Joseph. And he did with a flourish, starting with a drawing of a scale from one of his famous songs. And Joe, now a doctor, still has the autograph.

**Meredith Willson, composer of *Music Man*, in
Mason, Ohio, which he called "River City."**

One time I attended an Iowa vs. Iowa State football game when
Willson was honored for composing both schools' songs. What an
honor!

He received an Academy Award for the music in Charlie Chaplin's 1940 movie, *The Great Dictator.* As an Army Major in charge of the Armed Forces Radio Service, he teamed up with George Burns and Gracie Allen in programs for the military. This led to him doing the music for and being a regular guest on the *Burns and Allen* radio show, playing a shy man asking for advice about women. He was on a variety radio production called *The Big Show* hosted by Tallulah Bankhead. Whenever he spoke to the tobacco-induced low-voiced Bankhead, he began every sentence, "Well, sir, (ahem) Miss Bankhead…" He even wrote symphonies and recently his alma mater, Julliard, named a residence hall after him.

He died at 82 and my biggest memory of all was attending his funeral in Mason City on June 15, 1984. The hearse paused at each place of honor in his life—his home, the library, the pool hall and other places he made famous, and finally the cemetery. At each place singers in seasonal garb sang highlights from *Music Man* songs. You don't get memorable events like that every day.

Meredith was a perfectionist. Someone said that his most famous musical took eight years to complete with 30 revisions. Some 40 songs were worked into the final piece and, of course, most people remember "Seventy-Six Trombones." But what a task it must have been to incorporate the women singers into the cackling chickens. Wow! One of my favorites was "Ya Got Trouble" and here is a little excerpt.

People:
Trouble, oh we got trouble, right here in River City.
With a capital "T" that rhymes with "P" and that stands for Pool,

The Beatles...
Wow. Did I Write This?

I wrote a regular column for the *Star-Courier* in Kewanee, Illinois, where I was editor and publisher from 1954 to 1971, calling it "Not All Malarkey." One of my columns caught the attention of a friend, Dave Clarke. He wrote a story in our paper on February 13, 1964:

> Newspaper editor Jerry Moriarity, himself the father of several teens and preteens, wrote an editorial about the appearance of the Beatles in the Monday, February 10, 1964, *Star Courier* in which he called the Beatles "the biggest musical fraud of the generation." He went on to say, "For one who has survived everything from the Charleston to the Big Apple, Frank Sinatra and on down to Elvis Presley, we think the Beatles are the leastest—not the mostest!"

> Moriarity said, "We frankly admit we've been fascinated by their haystack hairdos and the delirious teenagers who squirm and squeal with every antic before the microphones, but with a $1.50 haircut they'd be hooted down at any hootenanny in the country."

Does anyone think I was a bit hasty in my judgment of the Beatles? After all, the Beatles went on to become the most successful recording act of the 20th century. Just think—they sold more than 106 million albums in the U.S. alone, more than any other artist in the century.

Maybe it was the haircuts, or lack of them, that turned me off. Maybe it was their admitted drug use. At least I was in agreement with Jack Paar, former television host of the *Today Show*, who called the Beatles' performance the "downfall of British civilization."

They called themselves the Beatles, so they said, because it was like the "beat of the drum" and "everyone was stoned enough to find it hilarious."

They began recording in 1960 and hit it big in 1963 with Meredith Willson's "Till There Was You" and "I Want To Hold Your Hand." Their first tour to America was in 1964 when I saw them.

Yes, it's true that Elvis Presley, who volunteered to be an undercover government agent for Nixon, told the President that he thought the Beatles should be banned from this country because of their admitted use of drugs.

The Beatles, of course, are responsible for the long-time trend toward longer hair on men and the short-time trend toward Nehru jackets for men.

Well, whoever said we are infallible?

Shortest Interview on Record:
Andy Rooney

While I am on the subject of things that have backfired, let me just mention the shortest interview I ever had.

For many years, a number of Ex-PRESS Club of Arizona members would travel to Phoenix from the Sun Cities area for the annual honors program sponsored by the Walter Cronkite School of Communications, when this organization would honor leading journalists annually.

On November 6, 2003, Arizona State University singled out Andy Rooney, essayist for *Sixty Minutes*. The program at the Biltmore Hotel attracted a record crowd.

About eight of us were seated or standing near a remote entrance before the dinner when I spotted Andy Rooney walking down our nearly abandoned corridor.

I asked, "Andy Rooney, we have a group of about eight Ex-press club members just ahead. Would you mind posing for a picture with them?"

The curmudgeon, without breaking stride or looking up, rather gruffly replied, "No."

I Knew "Mr. Wizard" When

Among my acquaintances was Don Kemske, Don Herbert, and Mr. Wizard. Oddly enough, they were all the same person.

Don Herbert Kemske and I were students at the same time at La Crosse State, which now is known as the University of Wisconsin-La Crosse. Somehow both of us qualified as freshman players in a college production. The name of the play escapes me, but it may have been *Elizabeth the Queen,* which not only starred Don but MacDonald Carey, who went on to movie and television fame. Don played "the fool" in that production, one of nine in which he appeared. He also appeared after graduation in a 1940 Coach House summer theater production playing opposite Nancy Davis, future wife of President Ronald Reagan. Nancy did not meet Reagan until 1951.

Don even then was a superb actor and I was about as lousy as one could be. He seemed even then to be destined for an acting career. Later he changed his name to Don Herbert and became the professional we all knew he could become. Herbert was added to the cast of the long-running prime time anthology *GE Theater* hosted by Ronald Reagan from 1954-1962 and future president. As that program's "progress reporter," Herbert filmed brief science segments designed to make viewers think of the sponsor, General Electric, as a futuristic, high-technology company.

But Don's greatest fame came as Mr. Wizard, who for many years starred on national television as a teacher and specialist in various chemical, electrical and unusual experiments. When I went to New York for a training seminar by the American Press Institute at Columbia University, I made it a point to interview Don at his television studio.

I arrived with a throbbing headache which I'll explain in the next piece, but my reception at the studio was unusual. When I said

I was Mr. Moriarity who was to see Mr. Wizard, everyone perked up. Members of the crew came up to greet me and treated me very courteously, unlike how reporters usually are treated. This reception was hard to believe.

But before Don Herbert could complete filming a segment, a black man came in and introduced himself to a crew member, and everyone popped to for him. Surprisingly, his name was Moriarty (probably without the second i) and he was to be the new producer of the show. That's when the others became less interested in me.

It was good to see Don again and he modestly spoke with me, a man who never forgot "the little people." In those days, he filmed "live" with no rehearsals or time to change anything that went wrong. He described the wondrous and enjoyable accidents discovered as they went along filming.

His show, *Mr. Wizard*, was on the air from 1951 to 1964. His family moved to La Crosse from Minnesota when he was eight years old and he graduated from Central High School in 1935. He then attended La Crosse State Teachers College where I met him and graduated in 1940. He had majored in English and general science.

He served as an Army Air Corps pilot during World War II, so he wasn't exactly the nerd he appeared as Mr. Wizard. He became a B-24 bomber pilot who flew combat missions with the Fifteenth Air Force, flying out of an Italian base. He was discharged in 1945 as a captain and had received the Distinguished Flying Cross and the Air Medal with three oak leaf clusters.

He acted in a children's show in Chicago on radio before offering his idea for Mr. Wizard to NBC in Chicago in 1951. His shows featured a boy or girl who assisted him in each experiment. He didn't try to be funny but was so educational, that many children tried to copy his experiments in their kitchens or garages.

After his show ended, he wrote several books and introduced further ideas for new shows such as *Teacher to Teacher with Mr. Wizard* sponsored by the National Science Foundation in the 1990s.

When he was interviewed the month before his death, he was asked who he had influenced. He said, "There have been so many over the years: doctors, scientists, engineers, science teachers, science reporters, on-air science TV personalities. Actually, I feel very fortunate that I was able to spark an interest in so many lives."

He often returned to La Crosse but the press took little interest in covering his visits. However, there was considerable coverage when he died recently on June 12, 2007, at the age of 89 of multiple myeloma.

America's Greatest Diarist: Edward Robb Ellis

My friendship with the world's greatest diarist, Edward Robb Ellis, started when I became publisher in Kewanee, Illinois, the hometown of Ellis.

He already had a great career as a newspaperman and started writing books. One of his most acclaimed books was *A Nation in Torment* about the Great American Depression, 1929-1939. I had contributed several articles of information, which he included in the book.

Later I became publisher of the Ottumwa Courier and our friendship continued. I worked to have Ottumwa named an All-American City and we produced a special publication, which I sent to Ellis in New York. That was in 1973 when Ellis responded with a very significant letter, which follows:

Dear Jerry:

What an edition! I know something about the time and talent and energy needed to produce such a massive and informative edition and so I congratulate you and all your staff.

You were correct in taking the viewpoint that every person is a story. News is people in action and history is action worth remembering.

I have been one year at the writing of *Echoes of Distant Thunder: Life in the United States, 1914-1918,* and have completed about half the book. After my literary agent read that portion of the manuscript he said it is even better than *A Nation in Torment.* I hope this is true. Although I enjoy my work it remains work, which means it requires the expenditure of energy and I am tired. To produce *Torment*, I consulted about 1,300 volumes; with *Echoes* I am using at least the same number of books.

I confess I am bitter toward a society that rewards lunacy and mediocrity, while letting its intellectuals and artists die. Trees are chopped down to make paper to publish pornography that makes some people rich. Men with enormous muscles are paid a million dollars for playing football. A television commercial advertises a car with the slogan: "Something to believe in." An automobile? What has happened to American ideals when we seek solace in things rather than ideas?

I write history telling youths about their national past so that they may understand themselves and understand society a little better, but all my time and all my energy and all my efforts are so ill-rewarded that before the end of the year I may be unable to pay my rent. I wish I could find an individual or institution or community eager to continue to pay my rent. I wish I could find an individual or institution or community eager to give me enough money for food and rent while I work my seven-day week producing something of value to everyone.

Creativity resides in solitary human beings, not in soulless corporations or impersonal government or swaggering unions. Silence and solitude are the matrix of creativity. The thinker is the carrier of culture. And unless Americans are willing to do something to save their artists they will lose their culture—which is committing suicide. I want to show in my books why we got to our present impasse. Never in history was there a nation that rose so high so fast, then fell so low so rapidly. Every single one of our institutions is under attack.

The young rebel—sometimes knowing why, sometimes not. The middle-aged subscribe to that famous American ideal: Buy more and more and become happier and happier. Materialists cannot be saved by things because things lack consciences and therefore are lifeless. A people can be saved only by learning to sense their inner spirit.

As a good Catholic you know the value of spirit—soul—call it whatever one wishes. Until I am cut down by poverty I shall try to show Americans their true soul.

Sincerely, Eddie

One time I spent a long, long evening with Edward Robb Ellis, who became the greatest living diarist in history (1911-1998). He wrote a page or two of notes for his daily diary, which started when he was a high school student and cheerleader in Kewanee in 1927 on a bet with two other fellows about who could write the longest diary—he won. Eddie was a reporter in Kewanee, New Orleans, Oklahoma City, Peoria, Chicago and New York but kept up his writing even when he was a featured writer for the *New York World-Telegram,* and after he retired.

The only time he was unable to maintain his diary was from 1942 to 1945 when he served in the Navy. Diaries were prohibited so he sent letters to his wife describing events and people—still very much like a diary. He and his wife divorced after his discharge— was it the impersonal letters? He regretted being unable to raise his daughter, Sandra, born in 1942, because of divorcing his first wife.

Eddie and I had met years ago in Kewanee when he came to visit his mother, who lived just a block and half from our home, and our friendship lasted until his death.

Jerry Moriarity with dapper Edward Robb Ellis

I was in New York to attend the American Press Institute at Columbia University, as I said before. When I gave him a call, he invited me to have dinner with him. He lost his dearest love, wife Ruth, to a heart attack in 1965. In later years, he dated women much younger. A long-time smoker, he was also suffering from emphysema. He became much larger and scruffier in older years, allowing his beard to grow long and white.

He and his female friend were excited about Italian wines and after (a long and wet) dinner we returned to his apartment, where shelves were lined with hundreds of his diary pages, which included his interviews with leading politicians and other dignitaries. Diary notes were so extensive that each volume contained notes for one year. His records also included tickets, invitations, correspondence, etc.

Ellis interviewed or had contact with such as Eleanor Roosevelt, Huey Long, Thomas Mann, Mae West, Harry Truman, Henry Ford, Elvis Presley, Frank Lloyd Wright, Margaret Sanger, Gen. Douglas MacArthur, Sinclair Lewis, Herbert Hoover, Grace Kelly, E. E. Cummings, and Irving Berlin. He also spoke with murderers, prostitutes, movie stars and failed suicide victims, and nobodies.

When "no comment" information was given him, he'd go to his typewriter later and write this critical information. Future historians will be able to glean pertinent and even damaging items from this great source of material.

Edward Ellis kept his off-the-record information protected until the deaths of his informants. He told me a number of times that he mentioned me in some of his diaries, so I became wary of saying or doing anything questionable.

After our Italian night on the town when we returned to his book-filled apartment, he and his friend broke out marijuana material and invited me to join in. I probably would have been tempted except I thought I'd end up in his diary again. So I declined. Watching them was like a transformation. The more they smoked their joints, the more they seemed to drift off into different worlds. This became obvious when Eddie got down on his knees and begged me not to tell his mother. I'll never forget that experience of a grown man so concerned about his actions when his brilliant mind became rather muddled.

The world's greatest diarist, Eddie Ellis, in his New York City home. He started his diary in high school in Kewanee, Illinois.

He also wrote books on the Great Depression, New York City, and suicide. In his book, *A Diary of the Century*, he explained that his diaries were to go to the Fales Library of New York University where they are now stored in a special collection. Others have written about him such as Laura Johnston's piece, "The Man Who Wrote the Century."

In 1995, a summary of his collections and caricatures was published under the title: *A Diary of the Century: Tales by America's Greatest Diarist.*

Perhaps his best work was *Epic of New York City: A Narrative History,* published in 1966 and republished in 2004. Ellis covered the four centuries of New York's existence, including such wonderful items as how the 1888 blizzard turned Macy's Department Store into a big slumber party. He also wrote *Echoes of Distant Thunder.*

Two years before Eddie died, I wrote him that my son, Joe, a medical student, had presented me with his book *A Diary of the Century* and how much I enjoyed it. I added the following words but never received a response from Eddie before he died.

Just this past summer I came across some old photos I took of you in Kewanee and you looked dapper as hell, not as bohemian as you probably do now.

At the time I never knew you were acquiring more conquests than John F. Kennedy. And I do believe accounts of your exploits, as documented in your diary, are correct. You must be tired.

According to your marvelous diary, you are an emotional person, often crying when events or impressions moved you. As a matter of fact, you were worried about me returning to Kewanee. With tears in your eyes, you got down on your knees and begged, yes, begged, me never to relay any of this (marijuana use and affairs) to your mother. At the time, I believe she was living in the Whiting House.

Obviously, I never did.

Do you ever feel there is something almost biblical about it when a person can be restrained from some questionable action, knowing it would be revealed? As it happened, your diary served as a guardian angel to keep me on the puritanical straight and narrow when you brought marijuana to our dinner for dessert.

Wish you could visit the Southwest so you could address the Ex-PRESS Club which I helped found with retired and present newspaper people.

Paul Ceynowa:
A Bonafide Marine Hero

A very remote relative, Paul Ceynowa, was and is a bonafide hero of Marine warfare in World War II. His brother was married to my wife's sister and we all had ties through Perham, Minnesota. Our close association with Paul remains to this day.

He was one of the Marines who survived the vicious assaults on Mount Surabachi on Iwo Jima. Many of his buddies did not. Paul was with the 28th Marines and he proudly points out that the 28th marines were the only ones involved in the famed hill, but his regiment had 1,300 casualties in the first day because the devastation of the Japanese defense was so intense.

Robert E. Allen wrote *First Battalion of the 28*[th] *Marines on Iwo Jima* and it was published by McFarland Publishing Company in 2004. Here is the section about Paul:

> Fearing a night assault, the company commander directed Paul Ceynowa to call for 81mm support against the enemy pocket. Recognizing the danger of mortar support in such a confined area, Sergeant Ceynowa positioned himself on a high point between the company and the enemy. In a calculated gamble, Ceynowa informed the mortar section of the exact location of the enemy and instructed the gunners to fire five rounds each. Any of the enemy not killed by the barrage sought refuge elsewhere, eliminating the threat of a night attack. p. 109.

A 2003 book entitled *Heartland Heroes* by Ken Hatfield published by the University of Missouri Press described the battle at Green Beach, Iwo Jima, on February 19, 1945, and included some information about Paul.

Sgt. Paul Ceynowa, a young forward observer for his 81mm mortar battery, First Battalion, 28th Marine Regiment, 5th Marine Division, reached the beachhead in the second wave. He said, "They made big use of the mortars...you don't hear them coming."

He was one of only ten marines that landed on D-Day to walk off the island under their own power....

Ceynowa said, "Binoculars drew sniper fire so we used them only when necessary...Flamethrowers were effective...when you hear those guys screaming with that stuff, burning alive, it was horrible to hear." P. 216-219.

Ceynowa was a forward observer with the rank of sergeant and he still is amazed that he remained untouched. Three machine gunners next to him were shredded. Paul had his communications man, Pfc. Clifford Matteson, remove their torn flesh and bone fragments from his helmet, backpack, and legs.

His unit lost three of its four officers the first night and out of 21 battalion commanders, 18 were killed or wounded in succeeding battles.

Paul gave me a note saying, "I've always looked for an explanation on who determines the great mystery of survival." One of his commanders observed, "Iwo was a graveyard for the dead and hell for the living."

To this date, Paul says a day never goes by without some of these experiences crossing his mind.

In 2007, Paul was one of four ex-servicemen selected to fly to Washington on an Honor Flight to view the War Veterans' Memorial. He was asked to write his account of the trip and submitted this letter:

Our Honor Flight to D.C. was such a grand experience. Our initial exposure to D.C. was the bus trip, which motored us to many historic buildings and sites. The driver of this bus was so informative with many timely humorous comments. We then proceeded to the Hyatt-Regency for check-in and the evening banquet dinner. We listened to a group of fine speakers topped off with an address by our special guest speaker, Sam Donaldson.

Our second day was a full day of viewing the great monuments in our nation's capital city, including the new WWII Memorial. We also viewed the changing of the guard at the Unknown Soldier memorial, along with the Washington Monument, Lincoln Memorial, Korea Memorial, Vietnam Memorial, Iwo Jima Memorial and the massive Arlington National Cemetery. I experienced a special feeling of gratification in viewing the flag-raising monument at the Iwo Jima Memorial. This monument is the greatest example of American valor in all of our military history. My regiment, the 28th Marine Regiment, was the only unit involved in the capture of Mt. Surabachi. I feel so fortunate to have survived this battle. I feel so honored to be one of the original, surviving members of the 28th Marine Regiment, which captured Mt. Surabachi at Iwo Jima on February 23, 1945.

The Iwo Jima monument was sculpted from the original photograph by Joe Rosenthal of the Associated Press. Since this event and photo was an authentic happening makes it very special tribute and gives our military a great sense of accomplishment and a grandiose feeling of pride and patriotism for our country. I'm so proud to have been a participant in this most gallant effort. May the Lord look after all of the many thousands who made the supreme sacrifice for our liberty.

Shoes of the Tallest Man in the World: Robert Wadlow

We wanted to see and hear Cab Calloway in his club in Harlem, but instead we got to view the shoes of Robert Wadlow, who the Guinness Book of Records listed as the tallest man in the world.

Wadlow was born in 1918, and by his death at 22 reached eight feet, eleven inches tall, just a fraction under nine feet tall. He weighed 490 pounds at his death in 1940, and was still growing, having suffered from hypertrophy of his pituitary (growth) gland.

It all came about during an Easter break from college, which then was called La Crosse State (formerly Normal and then La Crosse State Teachers College), but now the University of Wisconsin-La Crosse. This was in the pre-World War II era.

Because our family had a 1933 Plymouth, two buddies talked us into driving to New York with the offer that we could stay with this one friend during our stay.

Our friends were Francis Garvin (Bud) Duffy and Jack Sayer. Both are now deceased. Sayer, an Air Force pilot, was killed in World War II and Bud Duffy, one of my closest friends through grade school and high school, died in 2003. With proper tutelage, he could have been one of the nation's best tennis players—he had such natural talent.

During the trip east we had one problem. Duffy, then the driver, went off the road into a snow-covered embankment, and the car wouldn't move. So I got into the driver's seat, hoping to rock the car and free it, but it still wouldn't move. Here it was in the dead of night in the mountains of Pennsylvania and the transmission was out.

We started walking down the highway and shortly came upon a small inn that was open for breakfast. I never will forget the blueberry pancakes they offered. The owner lined us up with a garage owner and we started hitchhiking to New York in a snowstorm.

Sayer said he'd proceed first alone and Bud and I should stick together in order to catch rides. We lucked out because we were picked up by an official of the Pennsylvania Historical Society, who guided us on a grand tour, describing legends and myths incredible to hear.

Somehow we ended up near Delaware Water Gap and I can't even remember how we got to New York, but we did find Sayer's home and slept most of the first day.

Some of the Sprague family were our cousins. One was a big name in Tiffany's and another was a Donald Trump-like personality who, during the waning days of the Great Depression, supervised the reclamation of hotels.

When he offered to take us out on the city for dinner, we all hoped for Harlem because of the great entertainment there. Instead, we ended up at one of his hotels.

It was there he took us up to Wadlow's hotel room, but Wadlow wasn't there. We were taken into his room nonetheless and the size of his enormous shoes was pointed out to us. I believe they were size 27 but his last shoes were size 37 and are in a museum in Alton, Illinois, where he was born. The International Shoe Company made his shoes for free and he was a spokesman for them.

Wadlow had become famous because he traveled on a Ringling Brothers tour in 1936 and took another tour in 1938. The "gentle giant" as he was called, was the tallest boy scout in the world at age 13, and studied to be a lawyer but his health became too precarious to complete those studies.

While dining later, a gentleman came to our table. It was "Swing and Sway" Sammy Kaye, famous band leader, whose unit was playing there. Clearly, I was surprised later when the host's daughter asked if that man was a wrestler. And I, a relatively young Wisconsin college student, calmly set her straight. He was a handsome but tough look-ing guy, son of Czech parents, and his real name was Samuel Zarno-kay, Jr. He became famous for getting people up from the audience and giving them a baton to lead his band. We thoroughly enjoyed that evening.

On the 4th of July, 1940, while making a professional appear-ance at the National Forest Festival, a faulty brace irritated Wadlow's ankle, causing a blister and subsequent infection. Doctors treated him with a blood transfusion and emergency surgery, but his condi-tion worsened and on July 15, 1940, he died at age 22, the summer I graduated college. An estimated 40,000 people attended Wadlow's funeral. He was buried in a half-ton (1,000 pound) coffin that re-quired 12 pallbearers to carry, which was interred within a vault of solid concrete. It was believed that Wadlow's family was concerned for the sanctity of his body after his death, and went to these lengths of security to ensure it would never be disturbed or stolen. They also destroyed his clothing and personal effects to ensure that they did not become "freak" memorabilia.

His tombstone had the simple words "At rest." You might think that his tombstone would be the largest but instead that honor was given to someone named Daniel Moriarty (with one more i, he could be a relative) in Metairie Cemetery near New Orleans.

We still wished we could have seen Cab Calloway. You want to know why, don't you? He had been featured in the Al Jolson 1936 movie, *The Singing Kid.* His show at the Cotton Club in Harlem had become legendary, partly because he had started his career playing with famous Louis (Louie) Armstrong. And, I have to confess, I had just learned that his lyrics "kickin' the gong around" meant do-ing opium in Chinatown and "cokies" meant doing cocaine in his famous song, "Minnie, the Moocher," and "frail" meant a girl. Yep, I was a little naïve but my friends quickly filled me in.

Economics Giant:
Milton Friedman

Years ago, well, actually it seems to be light years ago now, I met a giant in the world of economics. And I am saddened because of the recent death of this giant, Milton Friedman, who succumbed of heart failure at the age of 94, November 16, 2006.

We met in Ottumwa, Iowa, when I was publisher of the *Courier*, the local daily newspaper.

I had initiated a campaign to have Ottumwa named an All-American City, and served as chairman of the planning group. I directed the preparation of the city's entry in the contest conducted by the National Municipal League and then I delivered the presentation to the All-America City jury, headed by Dr. George Gallup, in Denver, Colorado.

As a consequence, Ottumwa was selected as an All-America City and I received the Golden Throat award from the community, along with the Chamber's president's award. Some time during our celebration, we learned that Dr. Friedman would be coming to Ottumwa. We understood that he wanted to visit an honored community and expound on some of his economic theories.

When he came, we met him several times, and wined and dined what proved to be a fascinating individual. We wondered what his real purpose was in spending time in our community. While we did not understand or grasp completely his thoughts on the economy, we all recognized he was an intellectual. We did learn that he often advised Presidents Richard Nixon, Gerald Ford, and Ronald Reagan and presidential candidate Barry Goldwater. His influence spread to many foreign countries, especially Canada and Great Britain. I wish I had used a tape recorder while in his presence but I do recall some things.

He was very down to earth, even though I don't understand economics. Somebody asked him about greed and capitalism. He had a good answer—that there are no angels and that the world runs by self-interest, and we should "get over it."

I also remember that he and his wife Rose were in favor of parental choices for the education of children, with the capitalistic idea that the best schools should attract the best students.

He was born in Brooklyn to Jewish parents who lived in an area of Hungary that is now in the Ukraine. His father died when he was 15 but his mother and two sisters supported the family. They moved to New Jersey and he gained his degree from Rutgers University, then got a Master's degree in Chicago before going to Columbia University for doctorate work. He couldn't get an academic job so he went to Washington, D.C., where he obtained work under Roosevelt's New Deal. I found it fascinating that he criticized the government intervention programs that had helped him, saying all they had to do was to print more money.

Through the years, his views re-shaped capitalism worldwide. It is no wonder that he became a Nobel Prize-winning economist.

The Associated Press quoted President George W. Bush as saying, "Milton Friedman was a revolutionary thinker and extraordinary economist whose work helped advance human dignity and human freedom."

Even former British prime minister Margaret Thatcher, whom he strongly influenced, called him an "intellectual freedom fighter."

I was surprised to read that during his last year of life, he wanted to legalize marijuana. He and Eddie Ellis would have gotten along pretty well together.

Walter Mondale:
His Ticket Made History

Walter (Fritz) Mondale of Minnesota became vice president of the United States, but never succeeded in his campaign to become president. However, he did succeed in Japan where he was considered an "odmono." We'll explain later what that title means.

In his 1984 campaign for president, he did make history. Geraldine A. Ferraro stood proudly where no woman had stood before as she accepted the Democratic vice presidential nomination offered by Mondale.

With the two of them on the ticket, they hoped to wrest the White House from President Ronald Reagan. They did not.

When he spoke, Mondale saluted his running mate and targeted Reagan for a big loss, which never happened despite Mondale repeating, "I mean business."

Mondale later did become ambassador to Japan and did such a magnificent job that the Japanese considered him as an "odmono", a real honor meaning "a big shot."

By the way, we met Geraldine Ferraro when she joined Mondale in July of 1984 at a picnic event held in the backyard of his former home in the Minnesota border town of Elmore. As expected, it was a jam-packed event on the campaign circuit.

I was among those who were invited to the historic celebration of his 1984 campaign in Mason City, Iowa. That's the western Iowa community where Mondale appeared often and which he called his "lucky city."

Through the years we became well acquainted as he had been a carrier boy for the Globe-Gazette when he was a youth in Elmore, Minnesota, just across the border to the north. At the tender age of nine, he delivered our newspaper to 15 customers in his hometown of 880 persons.

In later years, he often visited my office in Mason City and I usually arranged paper throwing contests between him and several of our carriers.

One day on his first toss, he knocked a picture off the wall and the carriers howled in glee.

His campaign for the presidency was most exciting for us because he opened it and then closed his regional campaign in Mason City. He even provided me with a ticket for entertainment and refreshments November 5th at the North Iowa fairgrounds.

What I did not expect was that he escorted me to a place on the stage, which made me a bit uncomfortable as I tried to remain neutral. With my press camera, I tried to pose as a creative photographer from a great advantageous point.

In the ride to the airport after his talk, we had a far-ranging chat, not all of which was serious. After all it isn't every day one discusses that if he is elected, that he would choose me to be his vice president and my brother-in-law Don Gray (a Minnesota judge and friend of Mondale) to be the chief justice appointee. That gives you an idea how far the conversation drifted from reality.

When we asked if he'd be back if he's nominated, he quickly responded, "You bet, you bet. I promise it. I'll be back. This is my good luck city."

After turning west toward the airport, we posed the question, "What do you think of these analysts who are saying that if you don't finish a strong first in the Iowa caucus, you're going to lose and those who finish third are going to win?"

He answered, "I think those columns are worth every bit of the knowledge that went into them. First of all, nobody knows what the Iowans are going to do...People here don't push too easily."

In an easy-going exchange, he praised Iowa and his home state of Minnesota for promoting education with resultant high literacy rates.

Leadership: "Leadership requires several things we aren't getting. One, it's clear to me that this whole arms control effort has been botched and the situation in Lebanon is not getting any better. If you are going to lead the country, you have to start facing facts. That's the first thing for a safer world."

Priorities: "One, the need for a safer world; two, a more competitive economy; and three, a fairer nation."

Summits: After noting that President Reagan made a direct appeal to the Russian people, Mondale said, "That's a police state... That system isn't a democracy at all. That's why I want annual summit conferences."

Arms control: "It's interesting that Nixon, Kennedy, Johnson, Ford and Carter all got agreements to reduce arms and now we have nothing because instead of talking to each other, they've just hollered at each other."

Fitness: We asked, "How can you possibly keep in shape with the pace you've set and keep things straight, not just physically, but mentally?"

With a hearty laugh, he replied, "Who said I was in shape?" He added, "I try to get one day off a week where I can read, you know, and think and get my head straight."

Issues: "Tonight the reporters wanted to know and those farmers wanted to know about set asides, loan levels and such (about agriculture) and you better have answers. Next we go to Seattle and they'll want to know about Boeing Aircraft and I've got to be prepared at every stop to talk about the issues that concern them.

At the airport, Mondale lingered as the press corps, aides and Secret Service agents began boarding the waiting 747. He added more praise for North Iowa and his home state and reflected, "You know, I'd like to take those people up to Elmore or to one of the area high school basketball games to meet some more of the fine people around here...

Shortly he was on his way on another flight to another city for what probably seems an interminable round of talks, hand shaking and interviews, just as he had in his "good luck city".

PART FOUR

Not All Malarkey
Essays

Most Wanted to Believe

This story started out being almost unbelievable—and perhaps it was—although it captivated much of the attention of the world for months. This was the Necedah "vision" story.

When I was newly appointed state editor of the La Crosse, Wisconsin, *Tribune*, I picked up rumors about a gaunt, bespectacled farm wife, who claimed she was having visions of the Blessed Virgin Mary.

So I enticed the *Tribune's* ace photographer, Harry Larson, to join me for an investigation in the Necedah area, which then was on the eastern fringe of the *Tribune's* Wisconsin territory.

After a search we found the sand-entrenched farm land of Mrs. Mary Anne Van Hoof, who told us she expected to see her seventh vision of the mother of Christ on the feast day of the Assumption of the Blessed Virgin into Heaven. This was back in 1954.

The bespectacled Catholic mother of seven children told us she claimed to have seen and talked with the Virgin Mary on six other occasions and she claimed to have promises of two more apparitions.

Mary's special message, she said, was that the world should pray for salvation.

At the conclusion of our talk, she reached into her apron and withdrew a religious medal for each of us.

Our story attracted wide interest. Arrangements were made for special trains and buses from all points in the United States to accommodate the pilgrims, mindful of the fact that the church admits only that the Virgin Mary has appeared to a small number of devoted persons down through the ages, such as at Fatima, Portugal, in 1917.

Bishop John P. Treacy of La Crosse had issued a warning to Catholics that the Vision claims were extremely questionable. But hundreds of thousands attended, including the faithful and curious of many faiths.

The Catholic church did get involved in a negative way. The Necedah priest, the Rev. Sigmund Lengowski, pastor of St. Francis Church, who favored the visions, was transferred.

But there could be no belittling of the sincerity of the visionary herself.

She warned of prayer or destruction to Catholics, and to Protestants she said, "Remember your Lord in your way. Neither can Catholics carry on alone."

On the eve of the well-publicized event, Harry Larson, a tolerant, somewhat non-believer, and I took up our post on the sandy acreage, which already was filling at an amazing rate.

It was to be a sleepless night. As the sun sank lower, a loud speaker erupted with the first of hundreds, maybe even thousands, of rosaries (Our Fathers and Holy Mary's) almost to a numbing degree for hours and hours. There was no escape.

The crowd, which now included a delegation from Cuba, thickened to hundreds of thousands.

It became an overcast day, as I recalled.

I shouldered my way into the front row near the Van Hoof home.

Seconds later it seemed as though a miracle rush went through the crowd. Scores of followers pushed their way to the front, exclaiming variations of "It's a miracle," as they showed rosaries and other objects in their hands, claiming they had turned to gold. Hundred of the faithful claimed this.

When this frenzy eased up a bit, an elderly gentleman nearby said, "Any change taking place was just because of the perspiration occurring because of the excitement." He added that he was a doctor. But many in the audience still studied objects they held in their hands.

As I observed, it was a rather dull, dismal, overcast day.

And just as Mrs. Van Hoof was finishing an explanation of her vision, she raised her arms to the heavens and the sun burst through in full glory. With that, she collapsed.

With the help of family, including her husband, Fred, and others, she was rushed into her home. Fred expressed confidence that his wife does converse with Mary.

Daughter Joanne, 13, was prompted to ask her mother if she had seen the vision so she went inside and a moment later reported through the screen door as follows: "She says what a silly question—yes."

What attracted the huge crowd, close to 100,000? In my opinion, the tremendous crowd that flowed to the sandy farm home of the gaunt, bespectacled woman came in record numbers because they wanted to believe. And perhaps to regard this as a sign.

As I pointed out, her church had many misgivings about this, which it claims was unlike Fatima.

As a final twist, the Rev. Anthony Wagner was chosen by the La Crosse diocese to do a post-vision check and see if he and his committee could discover any credence to the Necedah visions.

Surprisingly, he invited me and a woman editor of a Catholic service in Washington, D.C., to accompany him on a late tour of the farm property. Obviously, we could not prove the visions were authentic. So the church's skepticism remains.

In later years, I delivered a number of talks on Necedah to various groups, but I am still perplexed by two incidents:

1. The timing of the sun's emergence just as she finished her talk and held up her hands to the heavens.

2. The tremendous outpouring of the huge audience who tried to prove their religious conviction and hope for reinforcement.

Obviously, it was a plea for rebirth of faith. Mary Ann died in 1984, but the movement goes on with extensive grounds, house of prayer, visitors' center, school for children, and items for sale.

At Least Religion Was Not a Major Issue

Fortunately, religion has not been a major issue in the 2008-2009 presidential campaign with more concerns about gender and race. It was a major factor when John F. Kennedy campaigned for president.

In one of my lectures for an Arizona State University-Sun Cities audience, I talked on this subject. Some of my thoughts were as follows:

Although Thomas Jefferson wrote most of the Declaration of Independence, a brilliant work (with its all men are created equal) he has been criticized for keeping his slaves. And he is quoted most often about separation of church and state.

Just as an aside, his own words did not mean religion should be ignored. In 1779, he advocated that state funds at William and Mary College maintain a 'perpetual mission among Indian tribes' and that they be instructed in the Christian faith.

When he was president in 1803, he sent a treaty to the Senate providing funds for a Catholic priest to Kaskaskis Indians.

His 'wall of separation between church and state' apparently was intended to preclude the government from establishing a religion such as in England. In fact, he favored free expression of religious beliefs.

Somehow, we are closer to views of the former Soviet Union, which banned all religious services, such as this country is doing in eliminating Merry Christmas in favor of Happy Holidays, and eliminating any expression in schools, including commencement addresses.

Although our government is isolating religion from the public sector, to their credit, Presidents Bill Clinton and George W. Bush have made more references to the deity than most of their predecessors. In more recent times, Gov. Douglas Wilder of Virginia raised the religious issue about Justice Clarence Thomas, asking how much allegiance he, as a Catholic, would owe to the Pope. The problem was that Thomas at the time was an Episcopalian, not a Catholic.

By the way, the first Catholic Supreme Court Justice was Roger Taney, who was married to an Episcopalian, Anne Key, Francis Scott Key's sister. They had a prenuptial agreement that all sons would be raised as Catholics and all daughters as Episcopalians. All six children were girls.

Let us hope that religious issues will be insignificant in the future.

Eight Minutes of Sunshine:
The Soviet Union in Transition

Back in November 1988, I had the honor (yes, even the pleasure) of joining a group of world journalists on a fact-finding delegation to the Soviet Union. This was before the breakup of the Soviet Union, but in the waning days of the USSR.

After my return I wrote an article entitled "Eight Minutes of Sunshine" which was reprinted in an anthology, *Big Ships Turn Slowly*. It was edited by Erin Bouma and published by the World Media Association in 1989 but is no longer available.

Somehow, my article received a healthy response so I would like to quote from it in part:

A somewhat dreary, snowy, freezing visit to the Soviet Union in November (1988) is not necessarily the ideal time in which to view a nation in a crisis mode. Yet, optimistic declarations in the world press about *glasnost* and *perestroika* had generated higher expectations and rosier hopes for the "democratization" of the vast monolith after three-score-and-ten years of Communistic rule.

But our reward was "only eight minutes of sunshine," ominously reflective of the dichotomous truth that the Soviet Union aspires to be a nation of hope, but remains a nation of despair.

The Mikhail Gorbachev era has been under way only three years, but his Western-style approach, while widely heralded in most international circles, has not been sufficient to propel the Russian people into the 20th century. Gorbachev is learning that the terms of *glasnost* (openness, free speech) and *perestroika* (restructuring) are easily described, but less easily implemented.

Passive opposition is coming from massive inertia of a people almost paranoid about change and from a bureaucracy protecting its own interests. More active opposition is coming from nationalistic and religious elements who desire reform or freedom, not stagnation.

Gorbachev's initiatives and efforts at radical transformation may not be rewarded with immediate success, but it is likely that the character of the Soviet society will bear his trademark as long as he bears his birthmark.

While disastrous economic policies have brought shortages of almost all foodstuffs and many necessities, Gorbachev's major accomplishment has been in reducing the threat from the outside world in the minds of his own people and in reducing the Red Peril in the minds of the outside world. Frankly, Gorbachev was masterful in his meetings with President Ronald Reagan and President-elect George H. Bush, in his globally telecast U.N. speech, and in his peace overtures to the nations of the West and the Third World. But his appearance camouflaged the deepening problems in his own country.

Cruel as it sounds, Gorbachev was the beneficiary of the awesome, devastating earthquake which snuffed out thousands upon thousands of lives in Armenia, where just days earlier brutal Soviet force was being called in to subdue demonstrators trying to escape the communistic yoke. Armenians and those in other satellite republics, principally Estonia, were seizing upon uncertain *glasnost* opportunities, which, if unbridled, could have led to the dismantling of the USSR. A little taste of freedom seldom satisfies, but the earthquake tragedy has temporarily softened the Armenian outcry.

Most of the Russians with whom we talked complained that economic conditions actually had worsened in the past three years.

How else can one explain people shivering in half-block lines just to buy hard-to-get coffee? Or lengthy lines to buy "mystery" meats or vegetables? Or Russians being denied entrance to Intourist hotels, where their own rubles are useless? American dollars are greedily sought.

We arrived in Leningrad after a Finnair flight from New York to Helsinki just days after the U.S. presidential election. Soviet journalists and others with whom we conferred liked Reagan and openly favored Bush, believing he would carry on Reagan's policies. But, as one Russian disarmingly acknowledged to me in a rare display of humor, "If you're happy, we're happy!"

Perhaps it would be best to summarize things I liked: The Kirov Ballet (my knees still ache from watching the magnificent leaps), black Russian bread (don't drop it or you'll break a toe), the Moscow circus (just like a Disney production).

Enjoying the Sights, Sounds
and Smells of Perham

I submitted this piece to the *Perham Enterprise Bulletin* and it was published November 21, 2002.

To the Editor:

We fell in love with Smalltown Minnesota when we settled in near Perham in Otter Tail County as we started, somewhat apprehensively, our retirement years.

But we believed then, as does the noted author of books and short stories, John Hassler, that "the small town is my life." And Perham, in the heart of the fabulous lake country, is the epitome of what is good and exciting about the state's values.

The sights, sounds, even smells vary through the seasons in Perham. In the fall, you can hear acorns pitter-pattering on heat-browned lawns, making one speculate uneasily about winter's early arrival. And there are the plaintive sounds of a mournful loon seeking his mate on a nearby lake. And sometimes hail stones tap dance on utility sheds. Later there are raucous chain saws cutting firewood to vie with snarling snowmobiles.

In winter there are apostrophes of icicles punctuating the eaves of homes. Undisciplined settlements of fish houses clutter ice lake surfaces nearby. And when winter gets serious, sparkling snowflake crystals softly descend, drawn to the twinkling outdoor lights until the warmed flakes dissolve into tears that languish on pine boughs.

In the city, wind chimes on a neighbor's porch provide an eerie accompaniment to seasonal sounds. And the pleasant sounds complement the fragrant smells of home cooking and baking, reflecting the heritage of the Germans, Polish and Scandinavians, who are rather dominant in this part of the Midwest.

Whether living in Perham during any of the four seasons, you have a great feeling of togetherness. Most people in our city know or know of their neighbors. It's a great place to be.

With more people employed by Perham industries than live in the city, the community has a reputation for progressive living. It has flourished while many others have withered on economic vines, prospering with its Tuffy's dog food plant, potato chip and chocolate factories, a modern Arvig Communication Center, huge elevators, a downtown filled with shoppers checking out many craft stores. And a sparkling community center, built solely through local contributions. Truly, this is the envy of visitors and officials of other communities.

Not to be forgotten are the International Turtle Races, held downtown weekly through the summer months. It is not unusual for young entrants from 20 or more states to be entered in the competition. There also are fine modern schools and a municipal 27-hole golf course, plus diamonds and soccer fields. Truly Perham is a great place to be.

An Irish Story for St. Patrick's Day

One of my favorite Irish storytellers from long ago was Jimmy Murphy, a sports editor from the Canton, Illinois, *Daily Telegraph.* We got acquainted when I was editor and publisher of the Star-Courier in Kewanee, Illinois. We often met at the Illinois State Boys Basketball tournament in Champaign.

Because of the scheduling, St. Patrick's Day always fell within the period when the Tourney was played. And Jimmy always was a star attraction in his all-green suit, which left no question about his heritage. He was almost as much an attraction as the players in the Sweet Sixteen, Elite Eight, Final Four and Championship games. Every year he'd get around to his special Irish story:

One day Father O'Malley spotted one of his parishioners, Patrick O'Brien, who had a taste for the forbidden beverage, his major vice. Father O'Malley decided to have a talk with Pat.

He advised Pat to take a pledge and suggested he give an offering to the Blessed Mother. "What do you suggest?" Pat asked. The priest suggested an offering of $2.50. Pat fumbled around in his pocket and finally pulled out a five-dollar bill. The priest tucked it into his own pocket, but did not offer the change. Then the two parted.

For several weeks, Pat kept the pledge. But one day as the priest sat in his rectory, he looked out his window and Pat was way out of control, stumbling from side to side.

At this point Father O'Malley decided to teach Pat a lesson so he clothed himself in a bed sheet and hid behind a tree until Pat wobbled into view.

The robed priest jumped out with up-stretched arms and proclaimed, "I am the Lord Thy God!"

Hearing that, Pat declared, "Well, go home and tell your mother she owes me two and a half ($2.50)."

Let Me Tell You About My Uncle Fred

On thinking back several decades, it is remarkable what a talented individual my uncle, Fred J. Bronsrud, was.

He married my mother's sister, the former Martha Krause, and for the most part of their married life they lived in the northern section of Minneapolis, Minnesota.

He was a veteran of some of the major skirmishes of World War I in France, but seldom discussed any of that part of his life. All we knew was that he went through hell. In later years, my uncle did relate how he had three motorcycles shot out from under him when he was a courier, relaying messages to the officers in the front lines.

We did hear once that he became quite a boxer for his infantry unit. He was a thin, but strongly muscled individual, probably in what would be a bantam class.

He once told me he was in a match with a naval opponent, who was coached by the former heavyweight champion, Gene Tunney. Uncle Fred had long arms of steel, which he sometimes almost wrapped around his opponent's neck while he hammered him with his right.

Laughingly, Uncle Fred told me how Tunney protested this tactic and my uncle invited him into the ring also, saying, "I'll do the same to you!" Who else would have had so much spunk?

A barber by profession, Fred could master almost any trade. He could be an electrician, plumber, carpenter, roofer, whatever. And he was competent in whatever he did.

But he surprised us with some of his other inventing activities.

For instance, he probably was the first to build turning signals for his automobile. He thought the idea was so great that he took it to patent attorneys. Their reaction: "They laughed their heads off," he recalled and yet today every car and truck does have turning signals. What an opportunity lost.

He had another idea...one to forestall robberies. That was in the days when cars had running boards. During one of his frequent journeys from Minneapolis to our home in La Crosse, he gave me a demonstration. He had an electric wire suspended through a washer connected to the car's horn. If anyone stepped on the running board, it would be set to honk the horn to warn the burglar off.

It was really an unusual device, a tribute to my uncle's creativity.

Legend of Deerman Persists

It seems incredible that after almost sixty years, the legend of Deerman comes to life. In the 1950s, a rumor persisted that a couple went to a lover's lane near the Johnson-Sauk Trail State Park just north of Kewanee, Illinois, and got a glimpse of Deerman. As a columnist for the Kewanee newspaper, I went to the site, saw both deer prints and a man's footprints in the road bed, enough "evidence" to write a fanciful account. So I created the idea of a silly Deerman.

On May 21, 2007, Dave Clarke of the *Star-Courier* resurrected my fanciful account of the half-man, half-deer creature who supposedly lurked in the woods near Kewanee. He was responding to a seventh grader who heard his parents discuss it. Clarke inquired of readers who might remember such a creature. People around the world including a Kewanee serviceman stationed in South Korea, who feared that the mysterious creature might track him down, wrote to Clarke. Some reported that if you saw Deerman three times, you would die. Here's Dave's column called "Seventh Grader Wants Truth About Deerman."

This writer recently received a letter from a Neponset seventh grader named Gus Block putting me on notice that the next generation wants some answers.

"I am writing this letter, Mr. Clarke, to ask for your help. My parents and some other old people I know have told me about a local legend known as Deerman. I am not sure whether to believe them or not. Some of the stories they have told me are pretty tall. As you are something of a local historian and have numerous contacts and sources for local facts, I feel you can uncover the real truth about Deerman.

"I am told your paper's editorial position is, 'the Deerman is malarkey.' However, I am sure you can approach this subject in an unbiased fashion and not disappoint me in responding to my inquiry."

Gus, your parents and "some other old people" were around back in the late 1950s and early 1960s when reports of something half deer and half man began to surface around Kewanee. I never quite understood whether the elusive beast had four legs like a deer and the upper torso of a man, or a man's two legs and the head of a deer, although I always assume the latter since no face was ever described. I, like yourself, was in grade school when Deerman was all the talk and, like you, only remember grownups talking about the mysterious creature.

Most sightings were reported in and around Johnson Sauk Trail State Park, north of Kewanee, although I believe there may have been some sightings on the north side of town.

One story I remember was about a couple of young lovers who were (ahem!) parked late one night on the road along Johnson's lake. Due to the activity inside the car (you know, talking and stuff like that) the windows were all fogged up.

All of a sudden, they heard what sounded like a hoof scratching on his window. The young man carefully rolled the window down a crack and peeked outside where he was shocked to see a half deer, half man lurking in the mist around this car.

I'm sure the *Star Courier* does not have an editorial position on Deerman. The legend comes up now and then and, like the black panther north of Osceola (which was real, by the way), we report what we hear, often with a disclaimer of any basis in fact.

I can tell you, however, that the Star Courier was instrumental in covering the first reports and that Deerman was, in a way "malarkey."

Back in the late 1950s and through the 1960s, the newspaper's editor and publisher was a man named Jerry Moriarity. There may be a few "other old people" around who remember him. (ouch)

Being of Irish descent, Jerry liked to tell tales in his weekly column, "Not All Malarkey." That is where the reports of Deerman first surfaced. I'm sure, like most things of this nature, the Deerman legend began with something someone saw—or thought they saw. Each time the tale was retold it grew a little bigger and scarier like stories told around a campfire.

Jerry fueled the mania by printing the latest "reports" of Deerman sightings in his column and, of course, sold a few more papers to a public now starving to know more about the strange beast.

The only physical thing about the phenomenon most people who were around then will remember was that "Deerman's" name could be found everywhere—signed to the back of road signs, across billboards, painting on the sides of barns—Deerman was everywhere. The graffiti continued to appear for many years, but has now disappeared.

Yes, I remember doing the story on Deerman well. It is difficult to believe the legend still lives so many years after I first wrote about the sighting. And I still remember vividly how a city auditor and former World War II Navy man, Harrold Monning, posted a huge billboard sign on the highway south of Kewanee saying "Mr. Malarkey is not Deerman." People had begun to think I created the legend and the signs so I should have been grateful to Monning.

Of course, the old idea of a creature half-man and half-beast goes back to the beginning of history and it obviously still has a great appeal. The Internet even has a "Deer Man's Chronicle Blog," and another site has a picture of a man dressed up with deer antlers. There is even a site called "Our Strange World" that described all the sightings years earlier by people who read Dave's Clarke's article and wanted to respond.

This is evidence to me, since I created the fanciful story from the report of the couple on lover's lane, that people are too suggestive and too ready to believe whatever they read. I never imagined that anyone would do more than get a good laugh out of my story.

Patrick's Question Will Linger

The following was written in tribute to the late Albert A. Gray, father of Elizabeth Jean Gray Moriarity, wife of the author.

* * *

"Why did Grandpa die? He was the bestest friend."

You're driving along the long, long road to northern Minnesota…on the sad mission that ultimately will take you and your family to the final rites for a beloved grandfather.

You glance over to the quiet-spoken, tousle-haired Patrick, who asked the question. How do you explain to a five-year-old about the death of his "bestest friend" or for that matter, how do you explain that to anyone?

The station wagon speeds ahead sharply as you press forward, passing a convertible load of laughing vacationers, oblivious to the sorrow that has struck the hearts of one family.

As you pull back into the line of traffic, you cast a glance again at the puzzled grandchild—your son—and cautiously grope for the right words.

You try to philosophize that God loves some people more than others and that He calls them to His side earlier; a quizzical look indicates the question—the "why" remains.

The engine drones on as you continue toward Little Pine Lake near Perham, Minnesota. This is the trip you have made many times before, but always under happier circumstances. Now you're going to "Grandpa's Lake" only this time he won't be there.

You reflect about the modern year-round home just recently built on the northwest shore. It was a lovely home which grandfather had been able to enjoy for only two weeks before being stricken with lung cancer.

Three months—three difficult months—had passed since he began his fight against impossible odds.

Your thoughts go back to the happy years shortly after your marriage…to Grandpa's favorite spot off Toad River where the big walleyes were biting "last week"…the friendly card games in which the in-laws such as me paid their "rent" in pennies…the succulent steak barbecues done with just the right touch over an outdoor grill…the picnic table which somehow always resounded to the cacophony of youngsters' cries, laughter and cheers which usually drowned out any serious adult conversation…until late at night when the children were bedded down.

And, yes, hand-in-hand Grandpa would proudly show off his garden with the ripening strawberries or other fruits and vegetables in season.

We remember, too, his patient vigil near the woodpile as he would wait with Danny and Mike or Kathleen and Mary Bridget for the curious chipmunks to venture out into the sunlight, noses crinkling at the summer delights about them.

How we sense the perishable splendor of nature; now we know he is apart from the transitory and evanescent world. Death is always tragic, have no doubt about that, but only in death can the soul be appeased.

How does one estimate the worth of an individual? Perhaps it is best not to try. The evaluation is for someone else.

We do know that the members of his family have a rich heritage in the memories of his life.

And maybe in time a more mature Patrick will find his answer in the death of his "bestest friend."

First Warning

The full impact doesn't hit you immediately.

At first, you're just a bit dazed, listening to probable causes, wondering what to do next, how to adjust. Besides, it can't be true.

Then several hours later as you rest between the crisp, clean sheets of the hospital bed, you notice you've been staring indifferently through the window, out at the cotton candy clouds and the bright sun being splintered by the trembling branches.

Outside the cheerful shouts of happy children echo and re-echo, but you find you've suddenly become apprehensive about gaiety. The sun shines brightly on, but strangely you try to keep it out, tightly jamming your eyes shut, leaving instead two fiery furnaces aglow and dancing wildly before you. Finally, the mist of an inner spring flows softly and the hot coals are slowly coals.

It is true! It has happened to you!

You've had the first signal that your body's timepiece, that throbbing, life-giving muscle you too often take for granted, is slowing down.

That happened to me, just last week after nearly a full week of extensive tests. And it was something we hadn't even anticipated… for there had been no signs.

Is this the same heart that carried our boyish feet over the rugged face of nearly every Wisconsin bluff along the Mississippi River? Is this the same heart that gave me energy to churn our arms in the long swim—almost daily—across the Ol' Miss in high school days?

Is this the heart that pounded so excitedly when we upset the defending city champion in tennis way back in '39 or so? Is that the same tireless perpetual motion machine that could keep our body treading water for more than an hour in Air Force water survival demonstrations during World War II?

Yes!

And it has happened to me.

Strangely enough, after the first jolting news, we now feel fortunate...fortunate to have a warning not everyone receives.

For one thing, it isn't as serious as it could have been. There are hundreds of others still thriving after severe attacks and we're led to believe our little disturbance is of a more minor nature.

Perhaps we will still get our quota of the three billion pulsations ticking off from birth to total surrender.

For a while, perhaps for a longer time, we'll have to ease up a bit. What the limits are, we don't know for sure.

But now we feel grateful to our God for the warning...for things again are placed in their proper perspective, in His pattern, according to His wishes.

Health Incidents

If I may, I'd like to relate a personal experience. I told it the first time to a group of college students in Illinois and I never expected to repeat it.

However, I did at my retirement after 50 years as a newspaperman.

Death to a child is mysterious, difficult to understand. My brother died when he was four and I was two. He was everything a mother could want, fair-haired, bright-eyed, loving. Whether it is something I actually did or heard about, back in my memory somewhere is the thought that I placed a rose bud on his casket. Memories play tricks so I could be wrong. It could have been one of his tiny friends. But I hope it was me.

As I grew older, I had a close friend in the neighborhood in my hometown of La Crosse, Wisconsin. We spent much time in his back yard. He had swings, chinning bars, plenty of pets, dogs, and even a pet crow.

His father took a great deal of interest in us, took us fishing on Pettibone Island, on camping outings and the like. It was no wonder that the home of my friend was so popular.

In contrast, my father was a railroad man, traveling every other day between Wisconsin and Minnesota. He was able to devote little time to his family, although he was very devoted to us all.

I'll never forget when my friend's father died and my dad took me to the calling hours in their home as was the custom in those days.

As we came out and were walking down the street, he asked me a question I'll never forget. He said, "He was more of a father to you than I, wasn't he?".

Whether I was choked with the emotion of the time or what, I could not or did not answer.

Oh, God, if I could just live that moment over, I would get down on my knees and say, "Dad, you're the greatest father a boy could ever want." But I didn't…and that moment is gone forever.

And now I am a father…of eight children, six sons and two daughters, and the grandfather of 16. All of our children have college degrees, but my prayer now is that they won't desire to aspire to be the richest people in the world, nor the most powerful, nor necessarily possess the greatest personalities. But rather that they all will develop into the men and women who can look at themselves in the mirror each day and see someone in whom they themselves can be proud.

If they can, perhaps then—and I emphasize the word, perhaps—perhaps then I won't ever have to ask if someone else is a better father than I.

Years ago when I gave a number of speeches, I often said, "If you don't know where you are going, any road will take you there." Most of you have made those choices and if you have, I hope you have helped others make those choices. Do it wisely.

In closing, I want to offer a suggestion for action in these difficult, but interesting, days. Francis Cardinal Spellman, who died a number of years ago, once said, "I shall pray as if everything depended upon God. I shall work as if everything depended on me."

Just Putting Away Some Memories

As the evening tiptoed away from the basement window, you stand alone among some cluttered memories.

A pile of dusty, yellowing letters, a wrinkled copy of a college newspaper, an aviation cadet insignia…yes, they're all there among others, many others.

Upstairs, a grandmother just home from the hospital fretfully and impatiently awaits the future, fearful perhaps of loneliness, apprehensive, no doubt, of inconvenience and dependence.

You've gone back home—for a day or two—and the past intrudes like a stranger, aloof and disdainful of the feigned maturity of one reluctant to "go back" in memory.

* * *

A passing car snorts to a start at the corner as it turns, the headlights chase around the basement rooms, dancing, frolicking, laughing and then they are gone.

* * *

You unpack another box. How quickly forgotten and yet how intensely interested we were in these back then. The letters, some of them are there—from friends already in service early in '41 and here's a rapid exchange as two of us tried to iron out a double date problem on a weekend…guess we both wanted to be with the same trim blonde. Funny though, I wouldn't even have remembered her name.

And over here are assorted photographs taken during, some after the war. Hmm! There's Errol Flynn in his smooth camelhair coat, looking belligerent as we accosted him for an interview in a Wisconsin snowstorm.

And, gulp, here's a picture taken from inside a glider, taken as we were jerked into the air by a plane at 165 miles an hour...you wouldn't catch me dead trying that today.

Wait! Who's this skinny kid? Not me, surely, but there's the name on a student identification card.

We dig deeper. A wrinkled flight cap with the proud Air Force emblem...four years gone...bivouac on an Arizona desert, but open post in Hollywood...freezing night flights with the bomb bays yawning wide, exposing the blurred fireflies of partially blacked out communities below...life snatched from boyish men...that seems so long ago now.

* * *

The cellophane wrapper crackles as it comes off, a match flares, the flame reaches the end of my cigar...a heavy line of smoke gropes upward to the bare light bulb and then flattens out among the tiny cobwebs of the basement rafters.

* * *

We turn back to our task. And here in a tiny box, a tiny garment, a boy's suit, placed away neatly with a mother's care. Ah, yes, how we remember—or do we remember only what we've been told—when we were two and he was four and someone gave me a red rose and I placed it on his casket. That was "Buddy," our older brother Daniel, an angel even then.

Poignant reminders—irreverently ripping open scars never really healed, exposing the turmoil, the tension, the temper of times past.

Suddenly the reverie is broken with the opening of the basement door and the clatter of our two daughters bursting downstairs, laughing and squealing.

"Oh, Daddy, look how dirty you are," Mary Bridget giggles.

We begin to repack the boxes, rearrange the mementoes, the letters, unable to discard them.

"What are you doing, Daddy?" Kathleen asks.

"Nothing, Honey. Just putting away some memories…just a few memories…let's, uh, go upstairs and tell Grandma that we'll clean the basement later.

Yes…much later.

Government Notifies You are Deceased...Gulp!

Admittedly you get a strange feeling when the government informs you that the Department of Veterans Affairs is sending out an official letter saying it has been notified of your death.

That was the first letter I received January 2004. The official notification was mailed December 18 to our homestead address in Minnesota, then forwarded to Fargo, North Dakota, and then relayed to Arizona, where we were spending the winter. The letter's journey took an extra 13 days.

What a way to start the New Year!

And it wasn't that the government said I was diseased, which may have been possible, but *deceased!* There is something final about that.

After sending letters to the Department of Veterans Affairs and to three Social Security Offices, this is what I learned:

1. My wife, Elizabeth, had survivorship benefits directly deposited into her bank in Minnesota.

2. My Social Security payments for three months had been returned to some Social Security office because, erroneously, I had been declared dead.

3. This all happened because we were spending the winter months in Arizona and had not monitored our Minnesota bank statements.

4. It turned out that some veteran died and my benefits were substituted for his.

5. Some people in Sun City West, Arizona, hearing of my plight, said I may have been a victim of identity theft, a possibility because Arizona then led the nation in such thefts.

6. Later I found how the transaction got fouled up. An employee of our Minnesota bank substituted my name for the deceased veteran, inadvertently, of course.

But that's just part of the story. A Social Security official outlined a procedure in which I was to contact an Arizona Social Security office in Glendale, Arizona, which I did.

I had hoped to be resurrected on the biblical third day, but it did not happen. I spent three hours that next day trying to convince the Social Security officials that I still had a pulse.

And my efforts to obtain a second Medicare card went for naught as I was told it hadn't been determined that I was not deceased.

Several days later, I had another call from the Glendale Social Security office, inviting me back, saying I had to return so a higher authority in the office could recheck my credentials and identity. And again I was rebuffed on obtaining a Medicare card.

And my "funeral" apparently went unnoticed because I did not hear of any tribute at my memorial service. The government never offered $250 for a grave marker nor have I, as a veteran, received an American flag.

However, through it all, I must admit that people in the governmental offices were courteous, competent, and pleasantly understanding. Now, sometime in the future, I hope to convince someone that I cannot find my military discharge papers.

Somehow I think I will fool them all. As I write this, I am ONLY 88 years old and I have two goals—the first is to live to be 93 and the second to reach 100. That should give me time to have my discharge papers come to light.

Postscript

After Death Story

The Day I Died

Note: During World War II, Lt. Gerald G. Moriarity penciled this article about an imagined event which remained hidden for more than a half-century.

I had often wondered how it was to die. And when it happened on the shores of Abangu, a short distance from Tubanku, it was amazing how easy it was to give up life...even though I wanted it so dearly.

No, I wasn't killed in action—just on a "routine" flight, the telegram said, months after the war had ended.

In the spring of '42, I entered the Air Force, of course, to be a pilot. First, it was Nashville for classification, then Maxwell Field in Montgomery, Alabama, for pre-flight, and finally Carlstrom Field, where we first tried out our wings.

It was in Arcadia, Florida, the night after I and four others had "washed out" that we sat around drinking beer, trying to convince ourselves that it was all for the best. Just because I crash-landed on my first solo didn't matter, did it?

Yes, we thought the check-rider was a stupe, that the Air Force was all wet and we really didn't mind a bit, although inwardly we ached...and we sought solace in suds, pouring down a few glasses to ease the pain.

And the next morning with a heavy heart, I remembered the beer glass with "Old Style" painted on it.

I had brought the glass from my home in La Crosse, Wisconsin, carrying it with me as a good luck piece. And it followed me everywhere after that.

How it survived all the thumping and bumping from field to field, coast to coast, is hard to understand. But it did, through Santa Ana, California, for a second pre-flight, aerial gunnery in B-17s in Arizona, bombardiering and navigation in New Mexico and then radar navigation training in Arizona.

Even my Chinese Nationalist students, when I was an instructor in Carlsbad, once sipped rum out of the glass—all except Yang Shou-tien, who was chosen the outstanding Chinese student trained in the U.S.

I was a radar navigator on B-29s in Kansas when the war was over as we awaited overseas shipment. And again the faithful glass was called upon, this time to toast V-J Day.

The next day those orders were canceled and our transfer went through to Arizona. On my delay en route, I stopped at my home in Wisconsin to place the treasured glass in a place of honor on top of the living room bookcase. It had served me well. I had survived the real war.

Our Arizona stay was short-lived and several weeks later our crew made the hop-skip-and-jump to Mather Field in California, then to Hawaii, to Kwajalein and finally Guam.

Johnny O'Brien, a flight engineer from home, was on the air strip when we ground to a halt that torrid afternoon and surprisingly enough was the first person I met though neither of us had been aware of the other's location.

Johnny, decked out with a couple of DFCs and air medals, citations and a Purple Heart, had had it rough—duty in India, Marianas and on the first aerial raid on Tokyo.

"About time you left the States," he kidded. "But then it's just as well. If the enemy had known what was coming, it would have held on a little longer. Yup, you stateside instructors had it rough," he smiled. "Let's check that Seagram's VO I've been saving."

Johnny left for home and a well-deserved rest several weeks after our reunion, as we prepared to photograph the numerous islands in the area.

I was in the radar compartment when the bail-out signal clanged out on our first mission.

"What's the joke, commander?" I asked the pilot over the interphone, but no answer came.

So I tugged open the pressure chamber door and was being blown through the narrow opening when a violent explosion rocked the plane.

A helpless feeling came over me and I wasn't certain if I were hurtling through the air or lying crushed against a bulkhead. Violet-amethyst stars sparkled just as though I had pressed my eyeballs hard when rubbing the sleep out of them.

The cold ocean water slapped me to consciousness even though I was dazed and hurt. My Mae West had inflated, but where my parachute was, if it had opened, I knew not.

In the distance, I blurringly made out a wooden spar of a sunken "Jap" ship and laboriously paddled to it, finally clutching the slimy board in almost a death lock.

That first cold night I must have slept for when a sharp pain jabbed my leg, I noticed the sun just rising.

Sea crabs were clinging to me and I tried to swipe them off. The hellish things were all over, cutting into my arms and legs, especially on my lower left leg. As I bent over to reach down, my head went under and the salt water rushed over me. "God, don't let me die, don't let me die." At last I was able to suck at the sky and fill my lungs.

My leg hurt more, excrutiatingly so, but I feared another ducking. It's like poising on top of a 1,000-mile vertical pipe, just waiting for it to draw me down to the ocean stomach and spew me out on the floor.

Each day was worse. This was the fifth or sixth or…guess I lost track of time…and my leg burned like a festering sore. As my hand groped down the shredded pants leg, I cried out, "Oh, God, no!" When I discovered my leg was shredded, too, hanging by strands or maybe it was the crabs pinching the crimson pieces together.

I've got to live. The sharks must have realized how greatly and deliriously I wanted to and they lazed respectfully in the near distance.

What seems light years later, my belly rubbed a sharp piece of coral and I shook convulsively, believing the sharks could wait no longer.

Another wave washed me closer to shore and jagged coral ripped my face from forehead to chin. And then I lay exhausted on the reef's edge, lapsing into a coma; only the slap-whish, slap-whish of the tide breaking the silence.

Hours later my eyes were weighted and dulled as they drooped open and there miraculously was a prayer's answer: A bird hobbled up and stood on my hand. Quickly I closed my fingers around it and tried to bring it to my mouth to eat, feathers, feet, head and all. Even alive!

My hand trembled and my mouth twitched and quivered. I rolled to my side in order to move my arm freely but as the bird flapped its wings for the first time I could see the pink spot on its wings. A pink spot! It was a blue-faced booby, but a rare booby, one of the last of the pink-spotted species, which some believed to be extinct.

But I can't care now, I must live. And as the bird is drawn closer to my mouth, my stomach revolts and I vomit painfully. I know I never could eat such an exquisitely beautiful creature. Slowly I open my hand and the bird steps out, preens itself proudly and nonchalantly stretches its wings.

Without this needed sustenance, my emaciated body gives up the ghost…and I die.

A startling whir of wings, frightening with its surprise, isn't heard by me, but a villainous vulture-type bird hurtles upon the pink-winged "sula dactylatra," cutting, ripping, splitting the dainty fragile bird, leaving it a throbbing, convulsive crimson mess on the sand and then with sudden distaste or disdain, without as much as even cocking its gnarled wrinkled head at its victim, flaps its massive wings, climbing higher, higher, and higher until it disappears from sight, all the while screeching raucously its throaty cacophonous death song.

And back in Wisconsin at home, my mother, reading the daily newspaper, hears the sharp ping and clatter of breaking glass and weeps in dread of the significance, afraid to look at the glass shards on the bookcase top.

Postscript: Fortunately, the death sequence never materialized. I wrote it with pens when so many of my Air Force buddies were getting killed over Germany or in the Far East. As is obvious, names of the islands and birds were written without reference to either atlases or bird books. This account lay unnoticed for years.

Lt. Gerald G. Moriarity in the U.S. Air Force in 1944.

About the Author

Gerald G. (Jerry) Moriarity was born in La Crosse, Wisconsin, on July 28, 1919. He homesteads at 44020 N. Little Pine Road in Perham, Minnesota, during the summer and 13039 Castlebar Dr., Sun City West, Arizona, in the winter. He is married and the father of eight children.

He was elected the outstanding young man of La Crosse, Wisconsin, Mr. Badger Jaycee of the entire state of Wisconsin, the youngest president of the La Crosse Business Men's Club, and editor of Racquet, the college newspaper, which was chosen an All-American publication. He was the director of the college publicity bureau, and winner of the Graf award as outstanding alumnas of La Crosse State College, which is now called University of Wisconsin—La Crosse.

He started full-time employment at *La Crosse* Tribune on St. Patrick's Day March 17, 1941, later becoming state editor of the *Tribune*. He was assigned to accompany Presidential candidate Harry Truman on a presidential campaign trip through Minnesota and Wisconsin, which started a chain of more than forty interviews and photo opportunities with all presidents from Truman to George W. Bush.

Before training as a pilot in World War II, he edited the aviation cadet yearbook, and as an officer, was an aerial and ground school instructor. He often said that if the enemy knew what was coming, it would have held on longer. He became a bombardier-navigator and aerial and ground school instructor; and was later a radar navigator in B29s. He trained Chinese Nationalist airmen including Yang Shou Tien who was honored as the outstanding Chinese student trained in the United States.

In Kewanee, Illinois, Jerry was President of the Association for Commerce and Industry, editor of the year of the entire state of Illinois, and head of the Illinois AP Editors' Association. He was also winner of the national and state contests for editorials, columns, and photography. He was a fourth degree member of the Knights of Columbus and winner of the Chi Gamble award in column writing, while being the editor and publisher of the *Star-Courier*.

Jerry's greatest personal victory was when he won a brawl with three newly promoted pilots in the Mission Café in Deming, New Mexico. He claimed it created the greatest excitement in New Mexico since Pancho Villa invaded Columbus, New Mexico on March 9, 1916. His base commanding officer requested a meeting with him for beating the "three biggest trouble-makers on base."

In Ottumwa, Iowa, as editor and publisher of the Ottumwa Courier, he brought international attention to the town of Ottumwa by creating 24-hour news and advertising on a leased cable channel. After being president of the Ottumwa Chamber of Commerce, he originated and successfully led a campaign to make Ottumwa the All-American City. This led him to create a campaign to make Ottumwa the All-American City. He was given the Golden Throat award for the campaign and chosen as Man of the Year for Ottumwa.

He also wrote an editorial in defense of Richard Nixon on Watergate that led to invitations to be a guest five times on the *All Things Considered* radio show.

In Mason City, Iowa, he published the *Mason City Globe-Gazette*. He was president of the Iowa Press Association, which merged two state press groups into the Iowa Newspaper Association. He leased cable channel for 24-hour news and advertising service, and built a TV studio in the newspaper. He then retired in 1984.

After retiring, he was given the Amos Award by the National Newspaper Association in 1995 as the outstanding community newsperson in the United States. He also received the University of Wisconsin-La Crosse Dr. Maurice Graff Award, the highest honor given to an alumnus. In addition, the Iowa Newspaper Association presented him with the Distinguished Service Award. He was Master Editor-Publisher of Iowa and Illinois Editor-of-the-Year.

The Supreme Court of Iowa honored him for service to the court as administrator of justice on the grievance commission, in a citation signed by nine justices. Iowa Governor Terry Branstad signed the citation for the State of Iowa, appointing him to the District Two Judicial Nominating Commission.

He was also the first newspaper man in the United States to lease a channel on cable television for 24-hour news and advertising services.

Story about me and cable TV advertising

He has given coast to coast talks and university lectures on the presidents, as well as writing and being the subject of numerous free-lance articles.

He founded the ExPRESS Club of Arizona, now called the Media Club of West Valley, for which he served as president three times. He was a guest at the White House many times.

He retired in 1984 after being editor and publisher of four daily newspapers in the Midwest. He described his motto as "Live your life, not just endure." The key to his longevity, he believes, is finding humor in everything and not taking life too seriously. "Everything doesn't have to be a crisis. A lot of people worry themselves to death," says Jerry.